Place Names

of the

Jersey Shore

Why Did They Name it That?

Southern Edition

LEE IRELAND

ISBN: 1439276692
ISBN-13: 9781439276693

Dedication

The inspiration for this book comes from my late father, Leroy Patrick Ireland. He was a truly exceptional individual. As a child he would take me and my sister fishing and crabbing. Sometimes, we rented a small boat with a low-power motor. We would wander through the back bays of Atlantic and Cape May counties. Here, he would point out the names of various places and explain the lore of their names and their origin (Along with a fish story or two). Vividly, I recall his explanations of places such as Methodist Ditch, The Mud Hole, Risley's Channel and the Mile Stretch.

❦ ❦ ❦

To

Best Regards,

Lee Ireland

CAUTION!

Do not use this book to navigate. While thoroughly researched and documented, this book does not include every place name nor is it intended to be definitive.

Request of Readers

While the name of every entry cannot be traced, other interesting naming and historical information is presented. Readers are kindly requested to contact the author at **Leeleader@comcast.net** with corrections, interpretations and place names to include in the next edition.

Table of Contents

About the Author

Lee Ireland is a lifelong resident of Atlantic County. He was born in Atlantic City and raised in Ventnor. His father, Leroy Patrick Ireland, passed on to him the folklore and history of coastal New Jersey. Some of this information can be found in history books and some cannot. Lack of documentation doesn't lessen its veracity. Lee has served his country through the nation's fire service for the last 40 years. He writes from his home in Egg Harbor Township with his wife, Regina and "At least two dogs."

A Note about Toponymy

What's in a name? Well, a lot, actually. In fact, everything is in a name. Naming something gives it meaning. That ultimate naming source, Linnaeus, said, "To know one thing from another, permanent distinct names must be given... recorded and remembered."[111] So, this book speaks to that which was meaningful to our ancestors and those who pioneered the Jersey Shore, lo, so many years ago. The place names are an important part of our heritage and the history of this area - so special to those who live here and those who visit our unique part of the state. It's a joy to share this information with the interested reader.

Note: The Apostrophe

Over time, the use of the apostrophe in place names has fallen into disuse. Michael Miller reported on this trend in his Press of Atlantic City, February, 2009 article. It is titled, "Has the apostrophe become dispossessed?" Miller stated that one reason for the elimination of the apostrophe is that cities seek consistency for their street signs. Societal customs and the "cut to the chase" syndrome, also tend to contract names as time goes on. This book reflects the trend and omits the apostrophe in primary entries since that is what readers will find on most signs.

New Jersey Forms of Government

All municipalities listed in this book fall into one of the following five types of government: 1-Borough, 2-Township, 3-City, 4-Town, and 5-Village.

✿ ✿ ✿

List of Townships by County

- **Atlantic County**

  * Buena Vista Township
  * Egg Harbor Township
  * Galloway Township
  * Hamilton Township
  * Mullica Township
  * Weymouth Township

- **Cape May County**

  * Dennis Township
  * Lower Township
  * Middle Township
  * Upper Township

Resources Used

- Geographic Coordinates are from "GNIS Feature Search." http://geonames.usgs.gov/pls/gnispublic/ f?p=116:1:337285432922406 2008, 2009 and "Lat-Long Finder." http://www.satig.net//maps/lat-long-finder. htm 2008 - 2010.

- Special thanks to the Atlantic Heritage Center, Somers Point, NJ, Richard Squires, President, for preserving Atlantic County's rich history.

- The web site; "COsports.com" proved to be an invaluable aid in the effort to easily state geographic coordinates.

- "Cape May County, New Jersey." Street Map Book. Alexandria Drafting Company, Alexandria, VA. 2002. Note: Most Cape May County entries' locales identified using this street map book.

- "Tidal stations Locations and Ranges" http:// tidesandcurrents.noaa.gov/tides09/tab2ec2b.html May 25, 2009.

- 196 - "Atlantic County, New Jersey." Street Map Book. Alexandria Drafting Company, Alexandria, VA. 2002. Note: Most Atlantic County entries' locales identified using thisstreet map book.

Place Names

Absecon Bay, Atlantic County. 39° 24' 31" N, 74° 28' 23" W. A 1992 Atlantic City Press story offered the explanation that Absecon is an Algonquin Indian word that means, "Little, on the other side of water."[2] See Absecon City entry.

Absecon Beach, Atlantic County. 39° 21' 51" N, 74° 25' 23" W. Once described as, "a 12-shack fishing village."[194] Absecon is an ancient Native American name meaning, "Little water."[39] Also see Atlantic City entry.

Absecon Channel, Atlantic County. 39° 23' 44" N, 74° 26' 00" W. Absecon is an ancient Native American name meaning, "Little sea water."[3] In 1989 it was listed as being a 120' wide by 7,000' long, channel across Absecon Bay. At that time it was planned to be dredged to seven feet deep at mean low water. The channel extended 700' into Absecon Creek. The dredging spoils were planned to be deposited at Black Point in Grassy Bay.[1]

Absecon City, Atlantic County. 39° 25' 31" N, 74° 29' 43" W. Absecon is an ancient Native American name. According to Sara Thompson-Smith in her book, "*A History of Ventnor City*," the Lenni Lenape Indians referred to this area as "Little sea water."[2] The Absecon tract of land was owned by Thomas Budd who sold tracts to the actual settlers.[112] Absecon has also been known as Peter White's Plantation, Mount Eagle and Absecum.[77] Absecon incorporated in 1872.[52]

Absecon Creek

Absecon Creek, Atlantic County. 39° 25' 13" N, 74° 28' 51" W. There are modern records of very large Striped Bass having been caught here. Absecon is an ancient Native American name meaning, "Little sea water".[3] Absecon Creek was first known as Reading River after John Reading the first owner of present day Absecon.[77] Also see Absecon City entry.

Absecon Inlet, Atlantic City and Brigantine City, Atlantic County. 39° 22' 33" N, 74° 24' 47" W. On early maps this inlet has been referred to as Graveford's Inlet and Graveyard Inlet.[130]

Absecon Island, Atlantic County. 39° 20' 38" N, 74° 28' 04" W. This is the Island that Atlantic City, Ventnor, Margate and Longport are located on. Absecon is an ancient Native American name meaning, "Little sea water."[3]

Adamstown, Atlantic County. See, "Pleasantville" entry.

Anglesea, Cape May County. 39° 01' 07" N, 74° 47' 42" W. A fishing village that eventually became North Wildwood.[41]

Its name derives from Anglesey Island which lies off the Welsh coast.[68]

Asbury Road, Ocean City, Cape May County. 39° 17' 05" N, 74° 34' 07" W. Ocean City was founded by Methodists. Asbury Road was named for one of Ocean City's founders.[40] This street runs virtually the entire length of the island, from Battersea Road at the North end, to 59th street in the south.

Atlantic City's beachfront from Ocean City's beach.

Atlantic City, Atlantic County. 39° 22' 39" N, 74° 27' 04" W. Named for the Atlantic Ocean.[51] Founded by Jeremiah Leeds.[40] Atlantic City Incorporated in 1854.[49] An old name for Atlantic City is, "Absecum Beach."[50] At one time or another, Atlantic City has also been known as, Further Island, Faraway Island, Absecon Beach, Leed's Plantation and Absecon Island.[77]

Atlantic City Reservoir, Absecon, Egg Harbor Township and Galloway Township, Atlantic County. 39° 25' 48" N, 74° 31'18" W. Located in Egg Harbor Township and Absecon but owned by the City of Atlantic City. It is surrounded by the FAA Tech center.

Atlantic County. 39° 28' 00" N, 74° 39' 59" W. The county was named by Daniel Baker, for the Atlantic Ocean. [51, 109] Atlantic County was formed On February 7, 1837 when Egg Harbor Township, Weymouth Township, Galloway and Hamilton Townships, split from Gloucester County.[52]

Avalon was once known as Leaming,
after Aaron Leaming who owned it in 1723.

Avalon, Borough of, Cape May County. 39° 06' 04" N, 74° 43' 04" W. Avalon is an Island in Welsh mythology and is located on Seven Mile Beach.[53] Aaron Leaming was the owner it in 1723. The first house, Old Limerick was built between 30th and 31st streets. Avalon Corson was the first child born on the island.[54] Avalon has also been known as Piermont and Leaming.[74]

Bader Field, Atlantic City, Atlantic County. 39° 21' 36" N, 74° 27' 22" W. Named in 1922 for Edward L. Bader, mayor of Atlantic City.[23] It was famous as an airstrip during the early days of aviation. First facility to use the term, "Airport" and also is the founding location of the Civil Air Patrol. Lindberg once used this field. Now a proposed casino site.[75, 82]

Bakersville, Atlantic County. 39° 22' 24" N, 74° 33' 17" W. Bakersville is the former name of Northfield. It was an early shipbuilding community. Bakersville was named for early settler, Daniel Baker, who operated a shipyard on the east side of Shore Road in 1814. By 1905 the name changed to Northfield.[55]

Bargaintown, Egg Harbor Township, Atlantic County. 39° 21' 45" N, 74° 34' 52" W. Tradition provides two versions explaining how Bargaintown was named. Perhaps most often cited is the version where early settler, James Somers, a large landholder, made a "bargain" with his slaves. If the slaves would build an earthen dam so he had easy access across a swamp, he would grant their freedom. Of course, the slaves would have to build the dam after a full day of work. The other version is from William Lake who stated in 1918 in his unpublished *History of Bargaintown,* that a loquacious blacksmith coined the name. The blacksmith, David Howell was very persistent in proclaiming the value of the lots that he had for sale, a real "bargain," to any customer who would listen.[56] Bargaintown was once known as Cedar Bridge.[77]

Bass Harbor, Somers Point/Egg Harbor Township, Atlantic County. See Lousy Harbor entry.

Beesley's Point, Upper Township, Cape May County. 39° 16' 36"N, 74° 38' 11" W. A ferry across the Great Egg Harbor River was established here in 1693, the year following the establishment of Cape May County.[137] Beesley's Point is the second-oldest resort in Cape May County, behind Cape May.[149] The famous ornithologist, Alexander Wilson spent four weeks here in 1813 studying water birds for the eighth volume of his *Cyclopedia of Ornithology*.[178] William Golden along with Rem Garretson, came to Cape May County around 1691. He settled on 1,016 acres at Beesley's Point.[139] Thomas Borden owned this land in 1803 when he sold it to Thomas Beesley who kept it until his death in 1849.[140] Dr. Maurice Beesley, presumably an heir of Thomas, was a famed historian of Cape May County, writing in the mid-nineteenth Century. Beesley's Point is also well-known for having accommodated the great John James Audubon during a bird-gathering visit here. Today, the well-known bridge that crosses the Great Egg Harbor River, join-ing Beesley's Point and Somers Point, is closed. Its fate is unknown.

Belcoville, Weymouth Township, Atlantic County. 39° 26'14" N, 74° 44'10" W. Belcoville is an abbreviation for "Bethlehem Loading Company." Belcoville came into existence to serve the military needs of the nation during World War I. Its pur-pose was to produce artillery munitions.[106]

Belleplain, Dennis Township, Cape May County. 39° 16' 07" N, 74° 52' 00" W. This town was originally named, Belle Plain.[149] Its name is a combination of two French words that mean, "Beautiful and plain."[60] Known to be home to prolific moonshine operations during Prohibition.[149]

Ben Hand's Thoroughfare, Upper Township, Cape May County. 39° 12' 14" N, 74° 40' 20" W. This waterway was named for a prominent family of settlers.[38]

Bennett, Lower Township, Cape May County. 38° 59' 00" N, 74° 54' 05" W. Bennett is one of several mid-nineteenth cen-tury communities that took their name from a local store owner.[141] There is a nature preserve here, Bennett Bogs, that offers examples of rare New Jersey plants. More pond-like, than bogs, over 250 species of plants have been noted here by the New Jersey Audubon Society.[107]

Betsey Scull Road, Egg Harbor Township, Atlantic County. See Betsy Scull Road entry.

Betsy Scull Road, Egg Harbor Township, Atlantic County. 39° 22' 03" N, 74° 42' 16" W. An alternate spelling is Betsey Scull Road. It is named after Elizabeth (Betsy) Scull. The road ran through her family's property where they operated a tavern, circa 1822.[225]

Bidwell Creek, Lower Township, Cape may County. 39° 07' 40" N, 74° 53' 29" W. This water feature is also called Bidwell's Ditch. It was dug by Richard Bidwell in the 1890s. Bidwell's Creek was formerly called Wills Creek.[204]

Bidwell's Ditch. Lower Township, Cape May County. See Bidwell Creek entry.

Black Horse Pike, Hamilton Township, Egg Harbor Township, Pleasantville, Atlantic City, Atlantic County. 39° 24' 52" N, 74° 34' 35" W. Possibly named for a tavern in Blackwood, NJ.[40] An historic road that runs through Atlantic County from the Gloucester County line to Atlantic City. At one time, it was a transcontinental highway going from Atlantic City, NJ to San Francisco, CA.[79]

Boardwalk, Atlantic City, Atlantic County. 39° 21' 31"N, 74° 25' 11" W. The Boardwalk is actually, a city street.[22] The first boardwalk was built by train conductor Alexander Boardman, and hotel owner Jacob Keim. Both men wanted to reduce the amount of beach sand that their businesses had to contend with. In 1870 they constructed a walkway made up of sections that could be removed in winter. By 1896 the walkway had been made permanent and was officially designated as the Boardwalk.[224]

Brigantine Beach Island, Atlantic County. 39° 24'07" N, 74° 22' 01" W. This island was known as "The Shoals" to New England whalers. These seamen built crude shacks on the beaches as they pursued their vocation.[3.5] It is also known as Ludleys Beach.[57] A brigantine is a sailing ship that has two masts. It is square-rigged except for the fore and aft main-sail.[3.75] Over three hundred sailing vessels wrecked in the vicinity of this island, over a 200 year period.[60.1] Long told, persistent rumors of buried pirates' treasure have always been centered on the island.[27] At one time or another, Brigantine Beach Island has also been known as Whale Island and Ocean Island. [230]

Brigantine City, Atlantic County. 39° 24' 49" N, 74° 22' 46" W. Named for a ship, a brigantine, wrecked circa 1710.[60] Formerly known as East Atlantic City. The city was connected to Atlantic City in 1924 by a toll bridge.[27]

Brigantine Inlet, Atlantic County. 39° 26' 47" N, 74° 19' 35" W. See Brigantine Beach Island entry.

Buena, Borough of, Atlantic County. 39° 31' 41" N, 74° 56' 41" W. Named for its good views and the 1847, Battle of Buena Vista, a major clash during the Mexican War.[172]

Buena Vista Township, Atlantic County. 39° 32' 23" N, 74° 52' 59" W. Buena Vista is a Spanish term for "good vision." It was introduced to the area after the Mexican War by George B. Cake, a local hotel owner, in 1848. In 1867 Buena Vista Township was formed when it separated from Hamilton Township.[160]

Burleigh, Middle Township, Cape May County. 39° 02' 44" N, 74° 51' 06" W. Burleigh was formerly called Gravelly Run. The West Jersey Railroad had a junction here and its name was changed in 1883 to honor John J. Burleigh of Camden City, NJ, a railroad entrpreneur.[205]

Butter Road, Upper Township, Cape May County. 39° 15' 33" N, 74° 41' 28" W. Runs from Tuckahoe Road to South Shore Road in Oceanview, NJ. This road led to a point where farmers shipped their butter to Atlantic City and Tuckahoe.[40]

Cape Island, Cape May County. 38° 56' 06" N, 74° 54' 22" W. Cape Island is the former name of the city of Cape May. In 1848 it was created as Cape Island Borough. It became Cape Island City in 1851 before becoming the city of Cape May in 1869.[81]

Cape May, cape. 38° 56' 06" N, 74° 54' 22" W (Cape May city). Cornelius Jacobsen Mey named this cape, Cape Mey after visiting here in 1622. He arrived aboard his ship, the "Glad Tidings," and named the south cape, Cape Cornelius. Today, we know the south cape as "Cape Henlopen." It is now part of the state of Delaware.[46]

New England Creek, home port to the whalers,
was dug out to create Cape May Canal.

Cape May Canal, Cape May County. 38° 58' 00" N, 74° 57' 47" W. lThe Cape May Canal was built during World War II to allow ships to enter Delaware Bay without the need to run the gauntlet of German submarines at the mouth of Delaware Bay.[4] New England Creek, where whalers once launched their craft, was dug out to create the canal.[34] Like many names at the Cape, it is derived from Dutch explorer Captain Cornelius Mey who explored the area in 1623.[34] The canal is a 1942 project of the U.S. Army Corp of Engineers.

Cape May, City of, Cape May County. 38° 56' 06" N, 74° 54' 22" W. The name derived from Dutch explorer Captain Cornelius Mey who explored the area in 1623.[34] Cape May was called Cape Island until the late 19th Century.[5] A resort city of renown, it is located at the tip of southern New Jersey.

Cape May County. 39° 09' 00" N, 74° 46' 59" W. This name derived from Dutch explorer Captain Cornelius Mey who explored the area in 1623.[34] Cape May County was already the home of Lenape Tribes such as the Tirans, Tiascons and Kechemeches when Europeans arrived. Explorer Henry Hudson visited Town Bank in 1609. The county was founded in 1850.[25] The Kechemeches ruled from Cape May Court House to Cape May Point.

Cape May Court House, Cape May County. 39° 04' 57" N, 74° 49' 26" W. Like many other places in Cape May County, this name came from Dutch explorer Captain Cornelius Mey who explored the area in 1623. It also derived from Daniel Hand who presented the county with an acre of land for government buildings in 1745. [34, 46] Cape May Court House was at first called Rummey Marsh, then Romney Marsh and later Middletown.[46, 74]

Cape May Point, Borough of, Cape May County. 38° 56' 14" N, 74° 58' 10" W. This is another name that honors Dutch explorer Captain Cornelius Mey. Mey explored the area in 1623.[34] Cape May Point was known as Stites Beach until 1876 when its name was changed to, "Sea Grove." A short, two years later, it incorporated as a borough.[99] It has long been rumored to be the site of buried treasure. The point is the proud home of the restored Cape May Point Lighthouse which was built in 1859.[46]

Cape May Court House was originally called Rummey Marsh.

Cape May Town, Lower Township, Cape May County. See Town Bank entry.

Cape May Turnpike. Middle Township & Lower Township, Cape May County. 39° 04' 37" N, 74° 49' 35" W. The Cape May Turnpike Company built a turnpike from Cape May Courthouse to Cape May in 1854. It ran roughly, along Route 9 and had toll houses at Cold Spring Harbor and in the vicinity of Cape May Courthouse. John Tomlin succeeded in building a road in the woods to the west of the toll road. This was a shunpike.[218] A 'shunpike' being a road created as an alternative to a toll road.[40]

Cardiff, Egg Harbor Township, Atlantic County. 39° 24' 36" N, 74° 35'14" W. When the first families moved to this area it was heavily wooded and a charcoal-making industry developed. It became known as Idlewood after the post office rejected the name of Cardiff.[113] Cardiff was named by a promoter of land development.[94]

Catawba, Egg Harbor/Hamilton Townships, Atlantic County. 39° 24' 25" N, 74° 42' 51" W. This is an unincorporated area that is located about three miles south of Mays Landing. The area was named by George West who, around 1810, donated an acre of land for the Catawba Methodist Church. It is speculated that the West family associated Catawba with their family history.[151] The dictionary defines the word as the language of American Indian people of the Carolinas and also as a variety of wines produced from a red American grape.

Cellar Creek, Upper Township, Cape May County. See, Corson Inlet entry.

Centerville, Galloway Township, Atlantic County. See Oceanville entry.

Chestnut Neck, Port Republic, Atlantic County. 39° 32' 21" N, 74° 28' 49" W. Chestnut Neck was once a town on the Mullica River that was home to Revolutionary War privateers.[28] It is located where the Mullica River, known as the (Little Egg Harbor River, at the time) and the salt marshes meet. On October 6, 1778 the village was burned to the ground by a British naval expeditionary force out of New York.[44] A 'neck' is a narrow stretch of land. Chestnut Neck is such a place jutting out into the Mullica River. Like all of Eastern America, the American Chestnut tree was prolific in New Jersey before the blight of the early 1900s.

Clarks Landing, Egg Harbor City, Atlantic County. 39° 34' 25" N, 74° 32' 25" W. Named for the Clark family that emigrated here from Connecticut during Colonial days.[112]

Clarkstown, Hamilton Township, Atlantic County. 39° 26' 06" N, 74° 42' 55" W. John and James Clark built seagoing ships here until 1872.[24] It is located approximately two miles NNW of Gravelly Run on the present-day Mays landing-Somers Point Road.[76]

Clermont, Dennis Township, Cape May County. 39° 09' 04" N, 74° 45' 46" W. Nearby, Leaming's Run Gardens features 25 themed gardens. Formerly named, Cressetown.[149]

Cold Spring, Lower Township, Cape May County. 38° 58' 00" N, 74° 54' 59" W. This spring gave its name to the nearby modern-day Cold Spring Village. The spring was located between the railroad tracks and Route 9, south of the village.[6] The spring was reported as rising in the marsh and being over-flowed at every tide.[143]

Cold Spring Harbor, Cape May County. 38° 57' 32" N, 74° 51' 57" W. Formerly known as, Two-Mile Beach.[50] Named after nearby Cold Spring.[143]

Cold Spring Village, Lower Township, Cape May County. 38° 58' 10" N, 74° 54' 48" W. Named for a nearby spring, Cold Spring Village is an authentic village that was established in 1973 with the purchase of Grange Building No. 132. Today it consists of a collection of 18th and 19th Century structures.

It is located three miles north of Cape May City between Route 9 and Route 626.[6]

Collings Lakes, Buena Vista Township, Atlantic County. 39° 35' 44" N, 74° 52' 54" W. The Collings Lakes area originally consisted of Cranberry bogs. The bogs were filled to make lakes.[72]

Collins Cove, Galloway Township, Atlantic County. 39° 32' 56" N, 74° 28' 29" W. This is a perennially popular spot for ice fishing. The cove is near Smithville on Moss Mill Road where Dr. Richard Collins had his Collins Mills. His family were early settlers of the area.[229]

Cologne, Galloway Township, Atlantic County. 39° 30' 17" N, 74° 36' 48" W. Cologne joins other towns along the White Horse Pike that were created as German agriculture communities. Its name honors the city of Cologne, Germany.[60]

Conovertown, Galloway Township, Atlantic County. 39° 26' 23" N, 74° 28' 43" W. Peter Covenhoven (Conover) was an early land owner whose name came to represent this unincorporated area.[60]

Corgie Street, Cape May City, Cape May County. 38° 56' 07" N, 74° 55' 04" W. Corgie Street is named for William Corgie, a Delaware River Pilot who owned a large tract of land in Cape May City.[40]

Corbin City, Atlantic County. 39° 18' 12" N, 74° 45' 21" W. Portions of Weymouth Township were taken to create Corbin City in 1922. It is located on the Tuckahoe River. Corbin City was once known as Champion's Landing and also as The Little City. During the Revolutionary War Bog Iron found here was sent to Aetna Furnace and then on to Batsto to be made into cannon.[173] Corbin City was also once named Tuckahoe.[50]

Corson Inlet, Cape May County. 39° 12' 20" N, 74° 38' 57" W. Commonly known as Corson's Inlet, it forms the boundary between Ocean City and Upper Township.[96] This inlet is named after John and Peter Corson, early settlers of the area. The brothers were Long Island whalers who anchored in the inlet around 1685. They dug a cave in a bank of Cellar Creek and lived in it during their first winter on the island. It was reported that the cave was discovered during the construction of the Garden State Parkway. Later on, the brothers erected a house. [25, 34] The inlet is known for hazardous sandbars that extend far into the ocean.[7.5] Variations on its name are; Corsons Inlet, Corstons Inlet, Cosiens Inlet and Costons Inlet.

Corson's Inlet. See Corson Inlet entry.

Corsons Inlet. See Corson Inlet entry.

Corson Tavern Road, Dennis Township and Upper Township, Cape May County. 39° 12' 19" N, 74° 42' 34" W. The road was named for the tavern operated by Amos Corson, an early settler of the area. Many early deeds referenced this road.[40]

Corstons Inlet. See Corson Inlet entry.

Cosiens Inlet, See Corson Inlet entry.

Costons Inlet. See Corson Inlet entry.

Cove, The, Ventnor, Atlantic County. 39° 20' 28" N, 74° 29' 08" W. This small bay off of the Mile stretch bordered Wissahickon and Monmouth Avenues. It is entered where West Canal and Inside Thorofare meet. Skiers, boaters and kids loved it. It contained seven hills, (probable dredge spoils) each separated by a creek. The author recalls that among neighborhood children, it was a mark of achievement to have hiked from Wissahickon Avenue all the way out to the seventh hill, to the west side of the entrance.

Cowpens Island, Ocean City, Cape May County. 39° 16' 56" N, 74° 35' 15" W. This island is located just southwest of Ocean City's 9th Street Bridge. It is a place where early settlers would graze their cattle. Being water-locked, there was no need for fences.[34]

Cox Hall Creek, Cape May County. 38° 59' 48" N, 74° 57' 26" W. Cox Hall creek was named for Dr. Daniel Coxe who purchased 95,000 acres of land along the creek from the Indians. Coxe, who was a physician to the English Court, hoped to develop a mercantile and agricultural community.[34] Coxe Hall Creek is also known as Bayshore Channel.[45]

Cresse Thorofare, Middle Township, Cape May County. 39° 04' 18" N, 74° 46' 41" W. In 1692 Arthur Cresse came from Long Island and was the head of a pioneering family in Cape May County.[108]

Crook Horn Creek, Ocean City and Upper Township, Cape May County. 39° 14' 23" N, 74° 43' 84" W. Looking off to the southwest from the 34th Street Bridge the pronounced curve of Crook Horn Creek is very evident and could explain its naming. This creek Separates Ocean City and Upper Township.

Da Costa, Hammonton, Atlantic County. 39° 36' 59" N, 74° 46' 30" W. Da Costa is an unincorporated area on the southeast boundary of Hammonton with Mullica Township. County Route 561, Moss Mill Road and US 30 run through it. Da Costa is "Old Hammonton." The first rail station was located here.[78] The highest point of land in Atlantic County lies within Hammonton along the Pennsylvania Railroad tracks.[181]

Davey's Lake, Lower Township, Cape May County. 38° 57' 05" N, 74° 57' 54" W. A nice hike will take you to this small lake where you may observe waterfowl if you're not too noisy. It is also called Davis Lake.[127]

Davis Lake, Lower Township, Cape May County. See Davey's Lake entry.

Delaware Bay. 39° 04' N, 75° 10' W. The Lenape Indian Tribe named the bay, Poutaxat. It was explored by English Captain Samuel Argall in 1610. He mistakenly thought that it was the northern limit of the Virginia Colony. He then named it after the colony's governor, Thomas West, 3rd Baron, Lord De La Warre.[34, 58, 60] Delaware Bay has also been known as Delawere Bay and Godenis Bay.[77]

Delilah Road, Hamilton Township, Egg Harbor Township, Pleasantville, and Absecon, Atlantic County. 39° 24' 52" N, 74° 32' 07" W. This road was created in 1829.[40] It is a major road that runs thru Hamilton Township, Egg Harbor Township, Pleasantville and Absecon. The origin for its name is unknown. One speculation has it that the road was named because the home of Theodore and Delilah Scull at the corner of Shore Road and what is now Delilah Road, was mentioned so frequently as a reference on deeds and maps of the mid 1800s, through the 1860s and 70s. In 1845, the road heading West at this intersection was called Delilah Lane.[8]

Delsea Drive, Dennis Township, Cape May County. 39° 07' 04" N, 74° 52' 00" W. The New Jersey State Legislature named this road Delsea Drive in 1933 because, at that time, it was the major road from the Delaware River to the Sea. It is also known as New Jersey Route 47. Delsea Drive is 75 miles long and runs from the city of Brooklawn in Camden County to Atlantic Avenue in Wildwood. It bears the distinction of being the longest state route in New Jersey.[83]

Dennis Creek, Dennis Township, Cape May County. 39° 09' 52" N, 74° 53' 44" W. Dennis is the name of a very early family of settlers who arrived in the Cape May area during its whaling days, the 1680s.[62] Circa 1802, this was the main port in Cape May County for shipping. Formerly a great ship-building community where at least 56 ships were constructed.[61] It is the site of Cape May County's first post office which was established in 1802.[142] It was home to a rum-running operation during Prohibition.[149] Dennis Creek was once known as Great Cedar Creek.[50]

Dennis Township, Cape May County. 39° 11' 00" N, 74° 48' 59" W. Dennis is the name of a very early family of settlers who arrived in the Cape May area during its whaling days, the 1680s.[62] The township was established in 1826 (government formed in 1827) from lands that formed the southern half of Upper Township. It contains the southern portion of Cedar Swamp. Today, Dennis Township consists of Belleplain, Clermont, Dennisville, Eldora, Ocean View, South Dennis, and South Seaville.[61]

Dennisville, Dennis Township, Cape May County. 39° 11' 35" N, 74° 49' 31" W. This is one of several place names derived from the "Dennis" family, the pioneering settlers who arrived in the Cape May area during its whaling days, the 1680s.[62] Dennisville was founded in 1726 by Anthony Ludlam.[133]

Diamond Beach, Lower Township, Cape May County. 38° 57' 34" N, 74° 51' 09" N. Located on Five Mile Beach.[87] Diamond beach's most notable feature is a long line of beachside hotels. It is sandwiched between Wildwood Crest and a wildlife management area at the southern end of the island. The beaches of the lower cape are the best spots to seek "Cape May Diamonds" which are Quartz crystals.

Dias Creek, Middle Township, Cape May County. 39° 05' 20" N, 74° 52' 50" W. Dias Creek was formerly named Dyers Creek in commemoration of the Dyer family.[50, 226] When applying for a post office, the name was spelled phonetically and that's how this town's name was changed. The Federal Writers Project reported that there was a healthy business of Horseshoe Crab farming conducted there. The animal was used as chicken feed and fertilizer.[86] During

President Roosevelt's New Deal, Dias Creek was the home of a Civilian Conservation Corp (CCC) camp. Later their camp became the headquarters of the Cape May County Mosquito Commission. Additionally, Dias Creek housed 200 German prisoners from Camp DuPont in Delaware in May of 1945.[206]

Dias Creek was once home to a thriving Horseshoe Crab industry.

Dorothy Volunteer Fire Company Station.

Dorothy, Weymouth Township, Atlantic County. 39° 24' 02" N, 74° 49' 26" W. Dorothy was originally part of Estelleville. Anderson Bourgeois was an attorney who married Anna Estelle, the daughter of the owners of the Estelleville colony. In 1897 he named present-day Dorothy, after his oldest daughter.[91]

Doughty Road, Pleasantville and Egg Harbor Township, Atlantic County. 39° 24' 60" N, 74° 32' 30" W. Named in honor of General Enoch Doughty, a lumber manufacturer. Doughty Road is a continuation of Marginal Road in Egg Harbor Township, east of the Garden State Parkway and runs to W. Park Road at the rail line in Pleasantville.[40]

Downstown, Buena Borough, Atlantic County. 39° 32' 23" N, 74° 57' 21" W. In 1774 the Methodist Church here was founded by Aguilla Down and Ambrose Pancoast.[72]

Drag Island, Somers Point, Atlantic County. 39° 17' 59" N, 74° 36' 59" W. This is an island consisting of mud from the dredging (*drag*ging) of area waterways.[34] Both the Garden State Parkway and Beesley's Point bridges pass over the island.[38]

Ducktown, Atlantic City, Atlantic County. 39° 21' 34" N, 74° 26' 32" W. This section of Atlantic City was settled predominantly by Italian families. They raised poultry and the area became known as Ducktown for the duck houses they built along the bays. It runs, roughly, from Texas Avenue to Missouri Avenue and from the bay to Atlantic Avenue.[100]

Dyers Creek, Middle Township, Cape May County. See Dias Creek entry.

East Atlantic City, Atlantic County. 39° 24' 49" N, 74° 22' 46" W. Former name of Brigantine.[27] See Brigantine City entry.

Egg Harbor City's Renault Winery maintains this attractive landmark.

Egg Harbor City, Atlantic County. 39° 31' 43" N, 74° 38' 53" W. This large area was settled by German immigrants. It was planned as a German agricultural community.[228] Egg Harbor City incorporated in 1858.[52] Famous Civil war General George McClellan asked, "Where's the harbor?" during his1877 visit. He stated that Arbor City was a more appropriate name, given the number of grape arbors he observed. Actually, the name came from the Mullica River which the town actually borders. The Mullica River was origi-nally known as the Little Egg Harbor River and back then, city planners had big plans for a water route between the city, Philadelphia and New York City.[227]

Egg Harbor Township, Atlantic County. 39° 23' 36" N, 74° 35' 35" W. Formerly known as Great Egg Harbor, the town-ship celebrated its 300th anniversary on January 2, 2010. Originally, Egg Harbor Township was part of Gloucester County and was even controlled, at one point, by Cape May County government.[65] The name is derived from, Eyren Haven; harbor of eggs. For name origin see Great Egg Harbor Bay entry. Also, see Cardiff, Bargaintown, Scullville, Farmington, McKee City, Steelmanville, English Creek and West Atlantic City entries.

Eldora, Dennis Township, Cape May County. 39° 12' 55" N, 74° 54' 22" W. Named in a contest held by a Mr. Dawson in 1892. Eldora includes the communities of East Creek and West Creek.[149]

Elwood, Mullica Township, Atlantic County. 39° 34' 35" N, 74° 43' 01" W. Elwood first went by the name of Weymouth Station. Like so many towns, it changed its name to avoid confusion when the first post office was established. It is named after Elwood Matlack.[158]

English Creek, Egg Harbor Township, Atlantic County. 39° 20' 57" N, 74° 40' 15" W. English Creek is located, "Five Miles up from the sea," on the Great Egg Harbor River. It was the

English Creek is the home of historic Asbury Church.

site of a boat building enterprise which produced two and three-masted schooners. It was named after early settlers, the English family. John English was the patriarch.[113]

Erma, Lower Township, Cape May County. 38° 58' 50" N, 74° 54' 29" W. Erma was formerly named, "Bennett."[207]

Estell Manor, Atlantic County. 39° 21'15" N, 74° 46' 24" W. This town dates back to a 1607 land grant from the king of England. It was named for the Estells, French Hueguenots who built a grand manor on the land and became important in the growth of the county. In 1837 John Estell built the Estell Glass Works into a main industry which produced for many years.[37]

Estellville, Weymouth Township, Atlantic County. 39° 23' 45" N, 74° 44' 50" W. Named for Daniel Estell, a founder of the town. He bought a window glass factory here in 1825. It employed 800 people and supported a village consisting of frame structures. It was formerly named Stevens Creek.[50, 37]

Farmington, Egg Harbor Township, Atlantic County. 39° 24' 25" N, 74° 32' 23" W. Almost named, "Marytown," for the housewives of that name, Farmington was chosen since the homes were on farmland, the rest of the area being woodland.[113]

Fishing Creek, Lower Township, Cape May County. 30° 01' 22" N, 74° 56' 02" W. A fishing fleet of as many as 100 vessels was reported as being anchored here by Lewis Townsend Stevens in his, "The History of Cape May County."[144] Fishing Creek is also the site (off Tabernacle Road) of the final resting place of 23 Black Civil War veterans.[29] Fishing Creek is also called Norbury's Landing.

Five Mile Beach, Cape May County. 38° 59' 20" N, 74° 48' 17" W. Also known as Five Mile Island[87,] this is the island that Wildwood is on. It is approximately five miles long depending on where you start and end measurement. A credible report exists telling of a sailing ship landing a party that retrieved a chest from the dunes before returning to the vessel. It has been documented that Captain Kidd visited the area.[46] A variation of the name is Five Miles Beach.[88]

Five Miles Beach, Cape May County. See Five Mile Beach entry.

Five Mile Island, Cape May County. See Five Mile Beach entry.

Five Miles Island, Cape May County. See Five Mile Beach entry.

Folsom, Borough of, Atlantic County. 39° 36' 07" N, 74° 50' 34" W. Folsom was originally called Wooley Field and then New Germany. In 1906 Folsom was created out of Portions of Buena Vista Township and named in honor of Franca Folsom, the wife of President Grover Cleveland.[155,156]

Ford Creek, Lower Township, Cape May County. 38° 57' 24" N, 74° 53' 27" W. Henry Ford I bought the land surrounding this creek for an automobile plant. It is named in his honor. Ford often spent his summers in the Cape May area.[34]

Forty Wire Road, Hamilton Township, Atlantic County. 39° 26' 21" N, 74° 45' 17" W. This short road runs between Route 40 and 11th Street. Some maps identify it as Walkers Forge Road. The naming of this road reflects common transmission practices from the early days of telegraphy and telephone communications. In the late 19th Century, with the spread of telephone service, new poles were erected to handle the wires. A series of poles had four cross-arms each that carried ten wires apiece. Hence they were known as '40-wire' systems. From this, came Forty Wire Road.[221]

Galloway Township, Atlantic County. 39° 31' 00" N, 74° 32' 59" W. Three origins of Galloway's name are offered. One holds that Galloway was named after an area of Scotland; Dumfries and Galloway or Galloway Mull. Another explanation is that it was named after Joseph Galloway a Loyalist delegate to the First Continental Congress. Finally, it is speculated that the name honors the Earl of Galloway Township, it being a king's grant. Galloway Township was a 1774 land grant from George the Third, King of England and the king of France.[2, 52]

Geneva, Atlantic County. Geneva is the former name of Linwood.[9] See Linwood entry.

Germania, Galloway Township, Atlantic County. 39° 30' 42" N, 74° 35' 58" W. This is one of several communities along US 30, also known as the White Horse Pike, that were established as German agricultural havens.

Goldbeaten Alley, West Cape May, Cape May County. See, Goldbeatten Alley entry.

Goldbeatten Alley, West Cape May, Cape May County. 38° 56' 12" N, 74° 55' 54" W. This narrow way was named after an establishment that beat gold to be used to line book edges.[40]

Golder's Point, Upper Township, Cape May County. 39° 16' 52" N, 74° 36' 55" W. See Beesley's Point entry.

Goshen, Middle Township, Cape May County. 39° 08' 29" N, 74° 51'11" W. Goshen was formerly named Cedar Hammocks.[149] This unincorporated area is named after the Bible's Land of Goshen.[129] Aaron Leaming first settled here around1693. In the second half of the 19th Century a thriving shipbuilding industry was located here on Goshen Creek.[128]

Gravelly Run, Hamilton Township, Atlantic County. 39° 25' 40" N, 74° 42' 21" W. This stream is a tributary of the Great Egg Harbor River. Around 1830, trading schooners transported products of area foundries, food and general cargo between Gravelly Run and Manhattan.[154] In more modern times it was famous for its swimming hole (typical Pinelands gravel beach with tea-colored Cedar water). A 'run' being a small stream. It was popular as the site of local high schools' Senior Day bashes.

Gravelly Run, Middle Township, Cape May County. See Burleigh entry.

Great Cedar Swamp, Cape May County. 39° 12' 13" N, 74° 46'19" W. The swamp terminates on one end, where the mouth of the Tuckahoe River enters the Great Egg Harbor River. The other termination is where Dennis creek meets the salt marsh of the Delaware Bay. It was not until Long Bridge Road, the current Route 550, was constructed, that the

Cape May area was opened up to travelers. A great source of lumber, the roof of Philadelphia's Independence Hall was made of wood logged in the Great Cedar swamp.[42]

Great Egg Harbor Bay, Atlantic and Cape May Counties. 39° 17' 29" N, 74° 36' 19" W. This name derived from Dutch explorers in 1614. Their journey southward along the coast brought them into contact with a land that teemed with bird life. The meadows contained many egg-filled nests. They named the region, Eyren Haven; harbor of eggs.[2]

Great Egg Harbor Inlet, Atlantic/Cape May Counties. 39° 17' 59" N, 74° 32' 44" W. See Great Egg Harbor Bay entry.

Great Egg Harbor River. Atlantic County. 39° 18' 15" N, 74° 38' 59" W. The Great Egg Harbor is a federally desig-nated, Wild and Scenic River. The name is derived from Eyren Haven; harbor of eggs. See Great Egg Harbor Bay entry.

Hamilton Bridge, Hamilton Township, Atlantic County. Hamilton Bridge is also known as Hamilton Village. See Hamilton Village and Hamilton Township entries.

Hamilton Village, Hamilton Township, Atlantic County. 39° 26' 55" N, 74° 43' 45" W. In 1756 John Hamilton purchased land on the south side of the Great Egg Harbor River. Over time, it came to be called Hamilton. It was located about a half mile from George May's Babcock Creek property. In 1837 Hamilton Village joined Mays Landing and was named the County Seat.[197] Hamilton Village is also known as Hamilton Bridge.

Hamilton Township, Atlantic County. 39° 27' 56" N, 74° 39' 59" W. Hamilton Township was formed in 1813 as a part of Gloucester County. Named after a surveyor whose name often was present on historic documents of the era, Alexander (Andrew) Hamilton.[2]

Hammonton was founded by Charles K. Landis.

Hammonton, Atlantic County. 39° 38' 11" N, 74° 48' 09" W. Hammonton was founded by Judge Richard J. Byrnes and Charles K. Landis. Their land sales attracted settlers from New England. The town was centered around a station named Hammonton for William Coffin's son, John Hammond Coffin.[158, 230] Hammonton has also been known as Hammon's Town and Coffin's Mill.[77]

Harding Lakes, Hamilton Township, Atlantic City. 39° 27' 09" N, 74° 45' 08" W. When U.S. President Warren Harding died in 1923, Harding lakes was a housing subdivision running along his, Harding Highway.[183]

Head-of-the-River, Estell Manor, Atlantic County. 39° 18' 42" N, 74° 49' 21" W. In colonial times this area was designated as the head of navigation on the Tuckahoe River. It is also called Head of River.[167]

Hereford Inlet, Cape May County. 39° 00' 55" N, 74° 47' 13" W. The 'Hereford' part of Hereford Inlet refers to Hereford, England.[63] Hereford Inlet is the site of the historic Hereford Inlet Lighthouse in the village of Anglesea, North Wildwood. A rum-running operation was known to be located here during Prohibition.[149]

Higbee Beach was a known rum-running spot during Prohibition.

Higbee Beach, Cape May County. 38° 57' 32" N, 4° 57' 54" W. This is a popular, somewhat remote, beach that runs along the Delaware Bay from Cape May Point to the Cape May Canal. It is famous as a bird watching site and infamous for being the site of nude sunbathing. Higbee Beach is named for the Higbee family. Joseph S. Higbee, a Delaware River ship pilot, began buying the land in 1823. The homestead remained in the Higbee family for over 100 years.[127] Higbee Beach was known to be home to a rum-running operation during Prohibition.[149]

Higbeetown, Galloway Township, Atlantic County. 39° 30' 55" N, 74° 27' 24" W. Higbeetown is an unincorporated locale in the general vicinity of Route 9 (New York Road) and Motts Creek Road. This area was named after the Higbee family who were early settlers of the county.[229]

Hildreth, Cape May County. See Rio Grande entry

Holly Beach, Borough of, Cape May County. Wildwood was formerly named Holly Beach. It was named in 1885.[33] In 1898 it was necessary to wade across Richardson Sound at low tide to enter the fishing village of Holly Beach.[10] See Wildwood entry.

Hope Corson Road, Cape May County. 39° 13' 12" N, 74° 41' 50" W. This road runs between Route 50 and Shore Road in the Seaville section of Upper Township. It is named for Hope Corson, a man, who was born in 1794. Over time, this name was given to both males and females of the Corson clan. He was a descendant of John and Peter Corson who settled the area. See Corson's Inlet.[195]

Indian Trail, Middle Township, Cape May County. 39° 07' 40" N, 74° 49' 22" W. Indian Trail was an authentic Indian trail used by the Lennai Lenape Indian tribe. They are a group that was in place in the area as Europeans found their way to these shores. This trail runs from Swainton to Goshen.[46] Today it is known as County Route 646.

Inlet, The, Atlantic City, Atlantic County. 39° 22' 25" N, 74° 25' 14" W. The Inlet is a section of the town that encompasses the northeast section of the Island bordering Absecon Inlet and the back bay. It is one of the most beautiful natural seascapes on the entire East Coast.

Ireland's Creek, Northfield, Atlantic County. 39° 21' 33" N, 74° 31' 33" W. Northfield was named by Daniel T. Steelman because a large part of the town was situated on the north field of a family estate.[174] The author recalls a Press of Atlantic City article that named the estate as that of the Ireland family. On an 1872 map by Beers, Comstock the creek is shown terminating on the property of a J. Ireland.[220]

Jarvis Sound, Cape May County. 38° 58' 02" N, 74° 51' 46" W. It's possible that this water feature was named for John Jarvis. There is a record from 1692 of Jarvis being convicted for giving rum to the local Indians.[34] Ironically, there is another record of a John Jarvis serving as a judge during the first court convened in Cape May County during March of 1693.[134]

Jeffers Landing, Egg Harbor Township, Atlantic County. 39° 19' 05" N, 74° 39' 07" W. This is the former name of present-day Scullville. This area was settled in the very early 1700s. The large Jeffries family were prominent in this area in early days. John Jeffryes II was wharf master of Jeffries landing in 1819.[113]

Jeffries Landing, Egg Harbor Township, Atlantic County. See Jeffers Landing entry.

Jenkins Sound, Middle Township, Cape May County. 39° 03' 32" N, 74° 48' 43" W. This sound was named for Nathaniel Jenkins, who, in 1712, founded the Baptist Church in Cape May Court House.[34]

Jim Leeds Road, Galloway Township, Atlantic County. 39° 28' 51" N, 74° 34' 11" W. A relative of Jeremiah Leeds, the founder of Atlantic City, is honored by this road's naming.[40]

Job Point, Egg Harbor Township, Atlantic County. 39° 18' 32" N, 74° 37' 50" W. Also known as Job's Point. The first officially recognized ferry in New Jersey ran across the Great Egg Harbor Bay between Job's Point (near Somers Point) Atlantic County and Goldin's Point (today's Beesley's Point) in Cape May County. Appropriately enough, Job Somers gets credit as the first operator. The ferry ran from 1693 until 1762. Job's Point acquired the reputation as an active rum running site during Prohibition. It is rumored that even today, bottles of whiskey can be found in the waters surrounding this popular water sports, fishing, crabbing and clamming, area.[11]

Job's Point, Egg Harbor Township, Atlantic County. See Job Point entry.

Jonathan Hoffman Road, Lower Township, Cape May County. 38° 58' 08" N, 74° 56' 20" W. Hoffman was a 19th century murder victim. The road formerly named Sunny Hall Road memorializes him. It is located just north of the Cape May Canal.[40]

Kimball's Beach, Middle Township, Cape May County. See Kimble's Beach entry.

King Nummy Trail, Cape May County. 39° 03' 41" N, 74° 52' 10" W. Today's County Route 618 (Indian Trail Road), is King Nummy trail. This is an authentic Indian trail that was used by the Lennai Lenape Indian tribe, a group that was in place in the area as Europeans found their way to these shores. This trail runs from Burleigh on Route 9 to Route 47, Delsea Drive.[46] Joseph Ludlam purchased present day Sea Isle City from King Nummy's Lenni-Lenape Tribe in 1692.[125] Records show that the Kechemeche Tribe (a branch of the Lenapes), led by King Nummy, preceded the New Englanders. There is a record that relates that the tribe sold a whale to an early settler in 1635.[30]

Lagoon, The, Ocean City, Cape May County. 39° 17' 36" N, 74° 33' 45" W. In this small and unique lagoon sits the proud home of the United States Coast Guard Ocean City Station. Its immediate proximity to Great Egg Harbor Inlet and the Atlantic Ocean makes it an ideal location for these maritime heroes. The author was once on board a craft that received a much needed assist from members of this station.

Lake Fred, Galloway Township, Atlantic County. 39° 29' 43" N, 74° 31' 58" W. Lake Fred is located on the campus of Richard Stockton State College. In years past, the lake had a reputation for attracting nude sunbathers. It is not definitive, but it is said that in the formative years of the Galloway campus that there was a student by the name of Fred who often was seen at the lake. He had a girlfriend named Pam, thus the name for the other lake nearby. Another version of the lake's naming says simply that students thought that the lakes should have names and randomly chose Fred and Pam.[210]

Lake Lenape, Hamilton Township, Atlantic County. 39° 28' 09" N, 74° 44' 32" W. This lake is named for the Lenni-Lenape (Delaware) Indian Tribe that inhabited the area prior to European colonization.[64] The Indians were members of the Unalachtigo branch of the tribe. The lake was an apple orchard prior to the 1847 construction of a dam across the Great Egg Harbor River.[197]

Lake Lily, Cape May Point, Cape May County. 38° 56' 20" N, 74° 57' 44" W. Local lore has it that during the war of 1812, American patriots dug a ditch from the lake to the sea in order to prevent the British from using it as a fresh water supply.[34] Perennial Lily pads adorn this well-visited body of water that plays host to tourists and wildlife alike.

Lake Pam, Galloway Township, Atlantic County. 39° 29' 43" N, 74° 32' 14" W. Lake Pam is located on the campus of Richard Stockton State College. In years past, the lake had a reputation for attracting nude sunbathers. It's not definitive, but it is said that in the formative years of the Galloway campus that there was a student named Fred who often was seen at the lake. He had a girlfriend named Pam. Other students started calling one of the lakes, Lake Fred and named the other nearby lake, Lake Pam. Another version of the name's origin says simply that students thought that the lakes should have names and randomly chose Fred and Pam.[210]

Lakes Bay, Pleasantville, Atlantic City and Egg Harbor Township, (West Atlantic City), Atlantic County. 39° 22' 18" N, 74° 30' 19" W. The name, Lakes Bay, refers to the Lake family. William Lake was a Long Island whaler who came into the region in 1690.[229] Simon Lake is a famous member of the clan who is credited with the invention of the submarine. Lakes Bay is also home to Lakes Bay Preserve which is one of the top windsurfing sites in the country due to its strong, steady winds.[184] The Ventnor Boat Works was located on the shores of Lakes Bay where the famed Ventnor speedboats were built. The Works also built many other types of boats in its lifespan which started in 1902 and lasted until the late 1960s.[185]

Lakestown, Atlantic County. See Pleasantville entry.

Landisville, Buena Borough, Atlantic County. 39° 31' 29" N, 74° 56' 18" W. Landisville is named after Charles K. Landis a developer who also founded Vineland and Sea Isle City. He planned to make Landisville the seat of a new county, Landis County.[164]

Leamings, Lower Township, Cape May County. See Rio Grande entry

Leaming's Run, Middle Township, Cape May County. 39° 08' 28" N, 74° 46' 00" W. Today, Leaming's Run is the home of Leaming Botanical Gardens. Twenty-seven different gardens run through a one-mile path.[46] Leaming's Run is named after the patriarch of all by that name in Cape May County, Christopher Leaming.[132]

Leeds, Galloway Township, Atlantic County. See Leeds Point entry.

Oyster Creek in Leeds Point maintains our maritime heritage.

Leeds Point, Galloway Township, Atlantic County. 39° 29' 31" N, 74° 25' 45" W. The pioneer, Daniel Leeds, West Jersey Surveyor General, is honored by this town's name.[64] Leeds Point was known, simply, as Leeds until 1844.[152] History tells us that Quakers, desiring to visit the Friends' meeting in Tuckerton, would swim their horses over the Mullica River from a place near Leeds Point. The place was called Swimming Over.[159] Leeds Point is the genesis for the legend of the Jersey Devil.[182]

Leedsville, Atlantic County. See Linwood entry.

Linwood, Atlantic County. 39° 20' 32" N, 74° 34' 12" W. Linwood had two sections, Leedsville in the north and Seaview in the south. The two joined to form the present day city.[2] At one time the town was named Geneva.[9,94] Shortly thereafter, "Washington officials" stated that to avoid confusion with other towns in America of the same name, that another name must be chosen. The "Early History of Atlantic County" states that "The ladies met in the school house and decided on Linwood."[93, 94] The name 'Linwood' may have been chosen in respect for the presence of Linden trees in the area.[95] Linwood has also been known as Leedsville and Pearville.[77]

Little Beach Island, Galloway Township, Atlantic County. 39° 28' 45" N, 74° 19' 31" W. This is the last completely undeveloped barrier island in New Jersey. It is also known as Pullen Island, North Brigantine Beach and Homer's Beach. Little Beach is part of the Edwin B. Forsythe National Wildlife Refuge. A life saving station was built here in 1894 and was occupied as late as the 1940s.[26]

Little Egg Harbor Inlet, Atlantic and Ocean counties. 39° 30' 16" N, 74° 18' 22" W. A direct land route from New York to Atlantic City was complete as far as Tuckerton to Little Egg Harbor Inlet. Funding for the final leg failed in 1932.[12] For origin, see Great Egg Harbor Bay entry.

Little Egg Harbor River, Atlantic County, This is the former name of the Mullica River.[44] For origin, see Great Egg Harbor Bay entry.

Littleworth, Upper Township. See Petersburg entry.

Longport, Borough of, Atlantic County. 39° 18' 51" N, 74° 31' 30" W. Although this is a long and narrow stretch of Absecon Island, it was actually named for John Long, the area's first land owner.[179] In 1913 Longport had a 1st through 10th street that, as a result of a storm, has become part of the North End of Ocean City.[13]

Lousy Harbor, Atlantic County. 39° 18' 53" N, 74° 35' 14" W (Bass Harbor). Lousy Harbor is a channel leading to Steelmans Bay. During the Revolutionary War, patriots captured the British ship, "Bellview" and brought her through the shallow channel. The ship's sailors were plagued with lice, as was commonplace at the time. Thereafter, the channel was called, "Lousy Harbor".[21] Lousy Harbor is also known as, "Bass Harbor."

Lower Township, Cape May County. 39°00' 57" N, 74°52' 41" W (Rio Grande). In 1723 Cape May County was divided into three precincts, "Upper," "Middle" and "Lower", Viewed on a map, "Upper" is at the top, "Middle," is in the middle and "Lower" is at the bottom. Incorporated in 1798, Lower Township is one of the state's original 104 townships. Cape May City was created from portions of Lower Township.[90]

Ludlam Bay, Dennis/Upper Townships, Cape May County. See Ludlam's Bay entry.

Ludlam Beach, Sea Isle City/Upper Township, Cape May County. 39° 08' 51" N, 74° 41' 40" W. This is the island upon which Sea Isle City and Strathmere are located. It is named for the Ludlam family who were early settlers of the area. The island is plagued with frequent, severe storm erosion.[14] Joseph Ludlam purchased the island in 1692 from King Nummy's Lenni-Lenape Tribe.[125]

Ludlam's Bay, Dennis Township and Upper Township, Cape May County. 39° 10' 39" N, 74° 41' 26" W. The bay is named for the Ludlam family, early settlers of the area. It is also known as Ludlam Bay.[34]

Ludlam's Beach, Sea Isle City/Upper Township, Cape May County. See Ludlam Beach entry.

Ludley's Beach, Atlantic County. See Brigantine Beach Island entry.

Malibu Beach, Egg Harbor Township, Atlantic County. 39° 18' 33" N, 74° 33' 15" W. Also known as the Sod Banks, a long popular surf fishing spot. In the 1960s the dunes made for a popular nighttime partying spot complete with bonfires.

Mankiller Bay, Atlantic City, Atlantic County. 39° 23' 54" N, 74° 26' 03" W. Located behind Atlantic City, it has long been known for very strong, "killer" currents that test mariners' strength and skills.[34] Another explanation of the name's origin comes from a longtime area boater and fisherman, Bill Killian of Absecon. He says the bay was named for the occurrence of large sharks there, large enough to ''Kill a man.''[35]

Margate, Atlantic County. 39° 19' 40" N, 74° 30' 13" W. In 1885 Margate was known as South Atlantic City. In 1908 the city renamed itself after a town in England. Home of the famous, Lucy the Elephant Hotel.[65] At one time, Margate consisted of three islands, an upper and lower section divided at Mansfield Avenue and a third island where the present-day western terminus of the Margate Bridge is situated, Pork Island.

Marmora, Upper Township, Cape May County. 39° 16' 00" N, 74° 38' 42" W. Formerly named Beesleys.[149]

Marshallville, Upper Township, Cape May County. 39° 17' 47" N, 74° 46' 07" W. At one time, Marshallville was a glass-making and ship-building town on the Tuckahoe River. Named for the Marshall family who operated a glass manufactory here.[208]

Martstown, Atlantic County. See Pleasantville entry.

Marven Gardens, Margate, Atlantic County. 39° 20' 01" N, 74° 29' 40" W. Misspelled, *Marvin Gardens* on the Monopoly game board, this is a housing development that borders Ventnor City. The author recalls riding a bicycle as a youth around the landscaped islands in the middle of the streets. The name is a combining form of the words **Mar**gate and **Ven**tnor.[165]

Mays Landing's Sugar Hill Inn, where privateers once dismantled British ships.

Mays Landing, Hamilton Township, Atlantic County. 39° 27' 08" N, 74° 43' 40" W. Mays Landing honors dock builder George May.[147] **In 1837** Mays Landing joined Hamilton Village, the same year that the seat of Atlantic County government was located there.[197] Samuel Richards and his wife donated property in Mays Landing to the Board of Freeholders for the county buildings on May 25, 1838.[52]

Several sources claim that Mays Landing was named after Cornelius Mey, the explorer. Mays Landing has also been called Iliff Town and The Landing.[74]

McKee City, Egg Harbor Township, Atlantic County. 39° 27' 01" N, 74° 38' 27" W. This development was the project of Colonel John McKee. McKee was the son of slaves and served in the Civil War.[222] He attempted to develop 4,000 acres that he owned that bordered the Newfield Branch of the Pennsylvania Reading Seashore Railroad.[31]

Methodist Ditch, Atlantic County. Located in the bay waters of Margate. Leroy Patrick Ireland told the author that back in the old days, it was common for some area ministers to make their living off the waters. He said that watermen, led by a local minister, gathered to dig this ditch in order to facilitate their travel as they worked throughout the wetlands.

Miami Beach, Lower Township, Cape May County. 39° 02' 04" N, 74° 56' 13" W. This is a coined name for a project that was built by the Miami Beach Builders Corporation of Philadelphia.[209] When we consider that at the inception of plans for the community of Villas that it was called, "retirement haven" and that North Cape May was referred to as "the St. Petersburg of the North," it's easy to see the mindset that existed for the naming of Miami Beach.[213]

Middle Township, Cape May County. 39° 03' 23" N, 74° 51' 01" W. In 1723 Cape May County was divided into three precincts Upper, Middle and Lower. Viewed on a map, Upper is at the top, Middle is in the middle and Lower is at the bottom. Incorporated in 1798, Middle Township is one of the state's original 104 townships.[101]

Mile Stretch, Ventnor, Atlantic City, Atlantic County. Road. 39° 21' 18" N, 74° 28' 22" W. This is actually Wellington and West End Avenues, an historic shortcut for traffic going between the mainland and down beach. During the author's youth two very tragic events occurred along this stretch of road. One was the head-on collision that killed two area building trades contractors. The other involved the drowning of several youths, most from one family, on the ice-choked bay despite the efforts of a passer-by who jumped in the water attempting to rescue them.

Mile Stretch, Ventnor, Atlantic County. Waterway. 39° 20' 49" N, 74° 29' 17" W. The annual Ventnor Regatta was held at Ski Beach, adjacent to this waterway, in the late 1950s. The author recalls that when the event was over that there was so much boat traffic leaving all at once in this narrow stretch of water that his 12' inboard felt like it was in the 'agitate' cycle of a washing machine.

Minnie Creek, Ventnor, Atlantic County. 39° 20' 20" N, 74° 29' 20" W. The author recalls catching bait for flounder fishing at the pump station located here on Newark Avenue between Plaza and Monmouth. A glass milk bottle loaded with white bread thrown from the bank with a string tied around the neck would produce results in mere minutes. Although it's not on any map that I know of, you could just ask any kid in the area and they would know exactly where you were referring to.

Minnie Creek, Ventnor Heights, Atlantic County. 39° 20' 50" N, 74° 28' 12" W. This site is offered by Thomas Klein, boyhood pal of the author and long-time Ventnor City official. This Minnie Creek is located just north of the Dorset Avenue Bridge.

Mizpah, Hamilton Township, Atlantic County. 39° 29' 12" N, 74° 50' 09" W. The name derives from the Bible and is translated, "God watch between us."[166]

Morris Beach, Egg Harbor Township, Atlantic County. 39° 18' 32" N, 74° 37' 50" W. The author was "First-in" on a house fire here during the 1980s. Later, grateful owners threw a steak dinner for the entire department. Mostly a summer community, it is located on Job('s) Point, the site of the northern terminus of the former ferry to Beesley's Point.

Moss Mill Road, Galloway Township, Atlantic County. 39° 30' 22" N, 74° 30' 19" W. James Morse had a mill on Mill Pond in Port Republic during Colonial days. Over time the name of the road that led to it became corrupted from Morse's Mill Road to Moss Mill Road.[110]

Mud Hole, Longport, Atlantic County. 39° 18' 35" N, 74° 31' 49" W. There were several hot fishing spots by this name in the 1950s. This one was about 30 yards from the jetty at Atlantic Avenue and 20th Street where the present day Church of the Holy Redeemer is located. Another spot by the same name is just off Malibu Beach in Egg Harbor Township on the other side of the bay. See Mud Hole, Egg Harbor Township, entry.

Mud Hole, Egg Harbor Township, Atlantic County. 39° 18' 44" N, 74° 32' 39" W. This is a well-known spot for Flounder fishing at the east end of the Sod Banks also known as Malibu Beach. It is just offshore of the entrance to a tidal creek and bridge on the Longport Boulevard. Another spot by the same name is just off the Atlantic Avenue jetty in Longport at 20th Street on the other side of the bay. See Mud Hole, Longport, entry.

Mullica River, Atlantic County and Burlington County. See Mullica Township entry. The Mullica River was formerly, named Little Egg Harbor River.[44]

Mullica Township, Atlantic County. 39° 36' 12" N, 74° 40' 40" W. Named for Finnish pioneer, Eric Palsson Mullikka.[66] Mullica Hill, NJ is also named after the explorer who once lived in Lower Bank.[122] Created from Galloway Township in 1838.[116]

Nacote Creek, Port Republic, Atlantic County. 39° 32' 29" N, 74° 26' 41" W. Nacote is believed to be of Lenni Lenape Indian tribe origin.[34] This waterway runs from the Mill Pond in Port Republic to the Mullica River.

Nesco, Mullica Township, Atlantic County. 39° 38' 17" N, 74° 41' 48" W. Nesco was formerly named New Columbia. The outlaw, Joe Mulliner was captured here at the Indian Cabin Mill Inn in 1781[122] Nesco is possibly derived from nearby Nescochague Lake, the site of a Lenni-Lenape Indian summer village.[123] Nescochague is derived from an Indian name meaning" wet meadow."[187]

Nescochague Lake, Mullica Township, Atlantic County. 39° 38' 09" N, 74° 39' 50" W. This is the lake that Pleasant Mills lies on. The lake provided power for an 1821 cotton mill.[48] Originally, a Lenni-Lenape Indian summer village, named Nescochague, occupied this site.[123, 153] Derived from an Indian name meaning" wet meadow."[187]

New England Creek, Cape May County. 38° 58' 01" N, 74° 57' 35" W. It is said that the early whalers from New England, launched their vessels here, circa 1640. This creek was dug out to create the Cape May Canal. See Cape May Canal entry.[34]

New Jersey. When asked, it is commonplace for people to state that New Jersey was named after an island in England. That is only fifty percent correct. Yes, Sir George Carteret named his lands in the New World in honor of the military defense of his home, the Isle of Jersey, but he named the province _West_ Jersey. Today's state didn't become **_New_** Jersey until it became a royal colony in 1702 when East and West Jersey were united and became the New, royal colony.[146]

Newtonville, Buena Vista Township, Atlantic County. 39° 33' 32" N, 74° 51' 58" W. Formerly named Penny-Pot back in the days when it was a stage coach stop or posting house.[156] Newtonville was named after a friend of Charles K. Landis. Newton had plans to develop the area.[72]

Norbury Landing, Lower Township, Cape May County. See Norbury's Landing entry.

Norburys Landing, Lower Township, Cape May County. 39° 03' 01" N. 74° 55' 40" W. Norburys Landing is also known as Fishing Creek. This is the site of the second oldest mill in Cape May County. It was a fulling mill which made homespun cloth. The mill was owned by Captain Richard Downs.[186]

Norbury's Landing, Lower Township, Cape May County. See Norburys Landing entry.

North Brigantine Beach, Atlantic County. 39° 25' 46" N, 74° 20' 21" W. Four-wheel- drive vehicles are used to surf, fish and recreate on this scenic stretch of beach. See Brigantine Island entry.[15]

Northfield, Atlantic County. 39° 22' 13" N, 74° 33' 01" W. Named by Daniel T. Steelman because a large part of the town was situated on the north field of a family estate.[174] The author recalls a Press of Atlantic City article that named the estate as that of the Ireland family. Northfield was once an oyster farming community and early ship-building community.[16] Originally called Bakersville for early settler, Daniel Baker, who operated a shipyard on the east side of Shore Road in 1814. By 1905 the name changed to Northfield.[55] Northfield has also been known as Dolphin.[77]

North Wildwood, Cape May County. 39° 00' 02" N, 74° 47' 58" W. North Wildwood's name alludes to an abundance of wild flowers.[171] Formerly, a small fishing village that went by the name of Anglesea.[41] Home of the historic Hereford Inlet Lighthouse.[46]

*Pioneer Jeremiah Leeds' grave is located
in a traffic circle in Northfield.*

Nummy Island, Cape May County. 39° 02' 11" N , 74° 47' 26" W. Nummy Island is the possible burial place of Lenni Lenape Indian tribe chief, King Nummy. There is a record of an Indian chief named Tom Nummi involving a 1685 land transaction.[34, 38]

Nummytown, Middle Township, Cape May County. 39° 01' 30" N, 74° 53' 47" W. Named for Lenni Lenape Indian tribe chief, King Nummy.[168]

Oberon, Margate City, Atlantic County. 39° 19' 27" N, 74° 30' 58" W. Oberon is a developed section of Margate that is roughly centered on Washington Avenue. Oberon consists of about ten city blocks from the ocean to the bay and is shown on an early map titled, "Map of Longport and Oberon."[85]

Ocean City was originally known as Peck's Beach after whaler John Peck.

Ocean City, Cape May County. 39° 16' 39" N, 74° 34' 29" W. Ocean City was formerly named Peck's Beach. John Peck conducted whaling operations from the island during that era and so it is likely that the area was named after him. Founded in 1879 by three brothers, Samuel Wesley Lake, James E. Lake and Ezra B. Lake and also William Burrell.[148] All four were Methodist ministers. Their intent was to create a temperance resort.[145] Ocean City has also been known as Pete's Beach, Pets and Peto.[74]

Ocean View, Dennis Township, Cape May County. 39° 10' 35" N, 74° 44' 01" W. Known to be home to prolific moonshine operations during Prohibition.[149] Home, at one time, to Van Gilders' tomato cannery at Magnolia Lake. Settler Aaron Townsend had a windmill erected here in the 1800s. The Shore Road and the route to Sea Isle City meet here.[211] The ocean is not actually in view, but one can't deny the smell of salt in the air.

Oceanville, Galloway Township, Atlantic County. 39° 28' 16" N, 74° 27' 38" W. Once known as Tanners Brook and prior to that Centerville. Indeed, a tannery was operated here at one time. It was reported that it took a full year to properly tan a cow hide.[112] Oceanville also has been known as Toadtown.[74]

Old Turnpike, Pleasantville, Atlantic County. 39° 23' 24" N, 74° 30' 48" W. This was the first (oldest) road between Atlantic City and Pleasantville. It entered Atlantic City on Florida Avenue.[16]

Old Turtle Thorofare, Cape May County. 39° 01' 24" N, 74° 49' 54" W. Old Turtle Thorofare is named for the preponderance of terrapins which exist to this day. Located behind North Wildwood.[34]

Otten's Harbor, Wildwood, Cape May County. 38° 59' 28" N, 74° 49' 42" W. This port is home to a large commercial clamming fleet.[41] Otten's Harbor was known to be home to a rum-running operation during Prohibition. One newspaper reported that a raid there netted, "...enough liquors, beer and wines... to fill a five-ton truck."[149] Named after Henry Ottens, around 1898. He was a land developer who is credited with beginning the boom that resulted in the development of Five Mile Beach.[150]

Palermo, Upper Township, Cape May County. 39° 14' 24" N, 74° 40' 21" W. Formerly named Corsonville.[149]

Peck Bay, Cape May County. 39° 16' 08" N, 74° 37' 20" W. Named for an early, circa 1700, whaler, John Peck.[34]

Peck's Beach, Cape May County. See Ocean City entry.

Penny Pot, Folsom Borough, Atlantic County. 39° 34'19" N, 74° 49' 20" W. Local lore has it that American Indians buried pots of pennies in this area that borders the Hamilton Township line.[162]

Petersburg, Upper Township, Cape May County. 39° 15' 13" N, 74° 43' 36" W. Once known as Littleworth.[119] Renamed in honor of local storeowner Peter Corson.[207] Pioneered by Abraham and John Vangilder.[138]

Petticoat Creek Lane, Lower Township, Cape May County. 38° 58' 18" N, 74° 55' 46" W. The name is derived from former Petticoat Bridge, a place where ladies were told to hang onto their petticoats.[40]

Pitney Road, Absecon, Galloway Township, Port Republic, Atlantic County. 39° 28' 18" N, 74° 29' 33" W. Named for Dr. Jonathan Pitney who pioneered the first railroad to the area.[40]

Pleasant Mills, Mullica Township, Atlantic County. 39° 38' 20" N, 74° 39' 39" W. A cotton mill was erected here in 1821. Earlier named Sweetwater.[77] The Elijah Clark mansion, also called the Kate Alesford Mansion, is located here and dates to 1762. Services are still held in Clark's 1758 Methodist Church.[48]

Pleasantville, Atlantic County. 39° 23' 26" N, 74° 31'07" W. Formerly named Adamstown. Two origins are suggested. The first explanation claims that Pleasantville was named by Dr. Daniel Ingersoll who was impressed by the surroundings.[187] An alternate explanation holds that Pleasantville is named after the store of Daniel Lake. Adamstown, Laketown and Martstown combined to form the borough of Pleasantville.[109] The grandson of one of the first settlers invented the first submarine. A USN submarine tender, the Simon Lake, is named in his honor.[17] Pleasantville has also been known as Risleytown, Lakestown and Smith's Landing.[77]

Pomona, Galloway Township, Atlantic County. 39° 28'42" N, 74° 34' 31" W. Pomona is the Roman goddess of fruits.[59] Pomona has also been known as Doughty Station.[74]

Pork Island, Egg Harbor Township, Atlantic County. 39° 20' 05" N, 74° 31' 19" W. Located on the Margate Bridge Causeway, behind Margate. Pork Island is home to the Pork Island Wildlife Management Area. This island was once was part of the City of Margate.

Port Republic, Atlantic County. 39° 31' 14" N, 74° 29' 09" W. Port Republic was originally named Wrangleboro by the Swedes who settled here in the early 1600s. By tradition, the name, Wrangleboro, came from the local taverns that were known for their raucous behavior. It became Port Republic at a meeting in 1840 when the citizen's first choice, Unionville, was rejected by the US Postal service due to a another New Jersey town having the same name.[28] Port Republic has also been known as Uniontown, Hewitttown, Clark's Mills and Tick Town.[77] It is also related that after the burning of Chestnut Neck during the Revolutionary War that its citizens moved upstream to the "Port of the Republic".[69]

Poverty Beach, North Cape May, Cape May County. 38° 56' 12" N, 74° 53' 39" W. Named for the type of grass present, Poverty Grass, which grows well in sandy soil.[117] Another explanation is that in the old days, the servants habituated this beach.[118] Poverty Beach is located at the eastern end of Beach Drive in Cape May.[216]

Pullen Island, Galloway Township, Atlantic County. See Little Beach Island entry.

Rainbow Channel, Ocean City, Cape May County. 39° 17' 32" N, 74° 35' 06" W. Rainbow Channel is located on the bays side of Ocean City. This channel is a perennial producer of Summer Flounder and Weakfish (Sea Trout).

Rainbow Islands, Cape May County. 39° 17' 58", 74° 35' 15" W. See Rainbow Channel entry.

Richardson Sound, Middle Township, Cape May County. 39° 00' 23" N, 74° 50' 26" W. Behind West Wildwood.[13] Named for a prominent family of settlers in the area.[38] In 1691 John Richardson was listed as a resident of the first town in the county, Cape May Town, (Town Bank).[135]

Richland, Buena Vista Township, Atlantic County. 39° 29' 30" N, 74° 52' 15" W. Richland was founded as a farming community along the railroad that ran from Newfield to Atlantic City by the Richland Development Company.[188] In exchange for $5,000 the Buena Vista Township Committee changed the name of Richland to Mojito for the first half of May, 2004. A sign on Route 40 was erected with the new designation. Local, Dalponte Farms is a major supplier of Mint, a major ingredient of Bacardi's mojito drink.[189]

Rio Grande, Lower Township, Cape May County. 39° 00' 57" N, 74° 52' 41" W. Rio Grande was once the hub of a thriving cane sugar industry.[34] There are several previous names for the town including, "Leamings," for the major landholders of the area and also, "Hildreth," for the people who ran the general store there. Aaron Leaming VII named the town after the famous river because it was pleasing to his ear. Compare this explanation with those locals who insist that the proper pronunciation is rye-o-grand.[84] Leaming was a descendant of the patriarch of all by that name in Cape May County, Christopher Leaming.[132] Rio Grande has also been known as Crandol Town.[149]

Risley's Channel, Egg Harbor Township, Atlantic County. 39° 19' 41" N, 74° 32' 14" W. The Risley family settled this in the area of this waterway.[190] The history of this area is that of a great maritime community.

Roaring Ditch, Dennis Township, Cape May County. 39° 10' 25" N, 74° 52' 40" W. Named for the tremendous rush of water during tide changes.[34]

Route 9, Atlantic and Cape May Counties. 39° 22' 45" N, 74° 41' 28" W. Route 9 roughly parallels the barrier islands throughout Southern New Jersey. As one of our oldest roads, it follows a long-established Indian path.[28]

Rum Point, Brigantine, Atlantic County. 39° 23' 00" N, 74° 25' 01" W. Located opposite the Atlantic City Coast Guard Station near the Brigantine Bridge. It is locally famous as a Prohibition-Era landing place for rum runners.[36]

Schellinger Landing, Cape May County. 38° 56' 56" N, 74° 54' 20" W. Named for an early settler family.[40] The patriarch of the Schellingers being Cornelius Schellinks.[132] This was a base for privateers during the Revolutionary War.[133] Known to be home to a rum-running operation during Prohibition.[149]

Scotch Bonnet Creek, Middle Township, Cape May County. 39° 03' 48" N, 74° 46' 49" W (Gut). A Press of Atlantic City reporter opined in a 1996 article that this geographic feature was named because of its shape, i.e. it looks like a bonnet.[34] The Scotch Bonnet is a seashell that is found along the East Coast.[36]

Scull Bay, Egg Harbor Township, Linwood, Atlantic County. 39° 20' 21" N, 74° 33' 10" W. The Quakers were one of the earliest groups to predominate eastern Atlantic County. Their plantations stretched along the Old Shore Road and Scull Bay from Nacote Creek to Somers Point. The Scull family was a prominent family during that era.[191]

Scullville, Egg Harbor Township, Atlantic County. 39° 20'06" N, 74° 38' 35" W. Joseph Scull (1826-1904), is the Scull family patriarch in the Scullville area. Joseph Scull II was his son and became postmaster of Scullville. Along with his family, Joseph II, ran a general store there. The author nearly fell through the roof of this building attempting to save it from fire during the 1980s. At one time, Scullville, was also known as Jeffers and Scull's.[113]

Sea Isle City, Cape May County. 39° 09' 12" N, 74° 41' 35" W. Originally named Ludlam's Beach.[108] Created from portions of Dennis township.[126] Founded by Charles K. Landis who also founded Vineland and Landisville, NJ. The town was laid out with canals inspired by the city of Venice, Italy.[125]

Sea Grove, Cape May County. 38° 56'14" N, 074° 58'10" W. Sea Grove is the former name of Cape May Point.[97, 99] Originally known as Stites Beach. Alexander Whilldin, a Philadelphia businessman, developed the Sea Grove Resort as a religious community. Surrounded by the sea and thick with trees, he gave it the name of Sea Grove. The land it occupied had been owned by his wife's family, the Stites', since 1712.[98]

Seaview, Atlantic County. 39° 19' 53" N, 74° 34' 08" W. Seaview is one of the few places along Shore Road, south of Pleasantville, where the ocean is visible. The back porch of Hagerty's Store, which later became a post office, was a vantage point.[109] See Linwood entry.

Seaville, Upper Township, Cape May County. 39° 12' 30" N, 74° 42' 15" W. Home to a circa 1727 Quaker meeting house located on Route 9.[214] From Seaville, there is direct access to the ocean via Mill Creek, Main Channel and Strathmere Bay. From there, it was out Corson inlet to the sea.

Seven Mile Beach, Cape May County. 39° 04' 22" N, 74° 44' 22" W. This is the land that the cities of Avalon and Stone

Harbor are located on. Today's island measures more on the order of 8½ miles of ocean front. Given shifting sands at both ends of the island and the tendency in old days to approximate distances, seven miles doesn't appear unreasonable. A name variation is Seven *Miles* Beach.[89]

Sewell Point, Cape May County. 38° 56' 38" N, 74° 53' 15" W. Sewell Point is home to the United States Coast Guard Training Center. A name variation is Sewell's Point.[97] The Coast Guard's historic tall-ship, Eagle, has been berthed here. General William J. Sewell was not only a Civil War veteran but also a recipient of the Congressional Medal of Honor. Sewell was a railroad magnate who filled in the marsh east of Cape May, built a hotel and bought Poverty Beach.[104, 170]

Sewell's Point, Cape May County. See Sewell Point entry.

Shelter Island, Atlantic County. 39° 21' 03" N, 74° 30' 00" W. Located behind Brigantine, it offers refuge for boats during foul weather.[34]

Shoemaker Holly, Upper Township, Cape May County. 39° 16' 27" N, 74° 37' 54" W. Located at Mile Marker 23 on the Garden State Parkway. Discovered during the construction of the Parkway, a rest area was created around the tree in order to preserve it, as it was in the middle of the highway. This is a 300-year-old Holly tree that is over 60 feet tall with a 30" diameter. It is located in a picnic area between the north and south lanes of the Garden State Parkway, three miles south of Ocean City Exit 25.[46, 161]

Shooting Island, Ocean City, Cape May County. 39° 16' 31" N, 74° 36' 24" W. Shooting Island is located just west of the Ocean City Municipal Airport. At one time, this was a popular place for duck hunters.[38] In recent times, the island has been used as a repository for dredge spoils. It was reported in March of 1989 that there was no more room on the island.[43]

The Garden State Parkway was relocated to save the ancient Shoemaker Holly.

Shore Road, Atlantic County. 39° 21' 53" N, 74° 33' 08" W. Known as the King's Highway in Colonial days, it is built over an

Indian trail. On a British map from 1769, Shore Road is the only road shown in what is now Atlantic County.[192] All roads from the mainland to the islands of the shore bisect Shore Road.

Shore Road, Cape May County. 39° 10' 14" N, 74° 44' 21" W. Shore Roads is also US Route 9 and runs from Beesley's Point in the North to the Cape May Lewes Delaware Ferry. The ferry is actually part of the route as it picks up again on the Delaware side.[217] Indeed, from this road, all the populated barrier islands in the county can be accessed.

Shunpike Road, Middle Township & Lower Township, Cape May County. 39° 00' 53" N, 74° 52' 36" W. A shunpike is a road created as an alternative to a toll road.[40] The Cape May Turnpike Company built a toll turnpike from Cape May Courthouse to Cape May in 1854. It ran roughly along Route 9 and had toll houses at Cold Spring Harbor and in the vicinity of Cape May Courthouse. John Tomlin succeeded in building a road in the woods to the west of the toll road, a shunpike.[218]

Simpson Avenue, Ocean City, Cape May County. 39° 16' 04" N, 74° 35' 45" W. Ocean City was founded by Methodists. Simpson Avenue was named for one of those founders.[40]

Sindia Road, Ocean City, Cape May County. 39° 17' 25" N, 74° 33' 50" W, Named in honor of the shipwreck that ran aground on Ocean City's beach.[40]

Ski Beach, Ventnor Heights, Atlantic County. 39° 21' 12" N, 74° 29' 14" W. This was a very popular place for water skiing during the 1950s and 60s. It also hosted the Annual Atlantic City Press Ventnor Regatta. The author recalls trying to 'rescue' a $10 bill tucked into the top of a greased flagpole during one event there.

Smithville, Galloway Township, Atlantic County. 39° 29' 38" N, 74° 27' 26" W. Smithville honors the Smiths who owned much property there. There was a hostelry/stage coach stop for the stage that came from Philadelphia via Camden located at Smithville.[112] Smithville was known as Leeds until 1844[152] and was also once known as Galloway Cross Roads.[77]

Snake Alley, Atlantic City, Atlantic County. 39° 21' 30" N, 74° 25' 41" W. Running between the beach blocks of New York and Kentucky Avenues, Snake Alley is the common name for the serpentine street that is officially designated as Westminster Avenue. It was once the nightlife entertainment center of the resorts' gay community.[219]

Snug Harbor, Ocean City, Cape May County. 39° 16' 56" N, 74° 34' 46" W. A small harbor located just north of the 9th Street Causeway. It really is snug, being tucked in between three streets and in the shadow of the 9th Street Bridge.

Socs Lane, Lower Township, Cape May County. 38° 57' 11" N, 74° 56' 09" W. Socs Lane is named for Socrates McPherson, a member of a prominent area family. Runs between Bayshore Road and Shunpike Road.[40]

Sod Banks, Egg Harbor Township, Atlantic County. See Malibu Beach entry.

Somers Point, Atlantic County. 39° 19' 02" N, 74° 36' 24" W. Somers Point is named for the Somers family who were early settlers of the area.[34] A port of entry was established here in 1797 when Somers Point was a part of Gloucester County.[154] According to an 1872 map by Beers, Comstock, and Cline, Somers Point was a part of Egg Harbor Township at that time. The map was installed in Somers Point City Hall during January of 1979.[18] Somers Point has also been known as Somers Plantation, Somerset Plantation and Somers Ferry.[77]

South Atlantic City, Atlantic County. 39° 19' 40" N, 74° 30' 13" W. Incorporated in 1885. In 1908 the city renamed itself Margate, after a town in England.[65]

The Somers Mansion has a commanding view of the Somers Point waterfront.

South Cape May, Cape May County. See South Meadows entry.

South Meadows, Cape May County. 38° 55' 53" N, 74° 56' 16" W. South Meadows was formerly named South Cape May. This is a beautiful, natural area that is well known for its outstanding bird watching recreation.[97]

Spicer Creek, Lower Township, Cape May County. 38° 56' 58" N, 74° 45'43" W. Spicer Creek is named for the Spicer family, early settlers of the area.[34] Jacob Spicer came from Long Island to Cape May County in 1691.[198]

Steelman Bay, Atlantic County. 39° 19' 10" N, 74° 34' 35" W. A name variation is Steelman's Bay.[21] James Steelman, a Swedish settler, had arrived in this area from Cinnaminson Township by 1865. He purchased 200 acres along Patcong Creek. A general store and post office were established here.[113, 187,]

Steelman's Bay, Atlantic County. See Steelman Bay entry.

Steelmanville, Egg harbor Township, Atlantic County. 39° 20' 03" N, 74° 35' 40" W. James Steelman, a Swedish settler, had arrived in this area from Cinnaminson Township by 1865. He purchased 200 acres along Patcong Creek. A general store and post office were established here.[113, 187] In early times it was commonplace for an area to be named after the family that operated the first general store in a locale.[109]

Stevens Creek, Weymouth Township, Atlantic County. See Estellville entry.

Stites Beach, Cape May County. Former name of Cape May Point and Sea Grove.[99] Alexander Whilldin, a Philadelphia businessman, developed the Sea Grove Resort as a religious community. The land that Whilldin developed had been owned by his wife's family, the Stites, since 1712.[98] See Sea Grove entry.

Stone Harbor, Cape May County. 39° 03' 03" N, 74° 45' 39" W. Located on Seven Mile Beach. Stone Harbor was created from portions of Middle Township. After the US Life Saving Service was organized in 1871, Station No. 35 was located in Stone Harbor, three and one half miles above Hereford Inlet.[202] The Avalon Development Company sold the southern portion to another company in 1907. It was called **Stone's** Harbor. The community of Stone Harbor was a creation of the Risley brothers, Howard, David and Reese.[203]

Strathmere, Upper Township, Cape May County. 39° 11' 44" N, 74° 39' 29" W. Strathmere is located on the northern end of Ludlam Island in Upper Township. Originally, Strathmere was named Corson's inlet. The name was changed to Strathmere

Stone Harbor was once the home of a life saving station.

around 1912, possibly, after the Strathmere Corporation; a land development company.[163] Approximately one mile off shore lays the wreck of a vessel that played a tragic role in maritime history. The General Slocum was an excursion steamboat that caught fire in 1904 causing the loss of over 1,000 souls. Almost all the victims were women and children when the disaster struck in New York Harbor. The boat was beached and later converted to a barge, the Maryland. In 1911 it sprang a leak as it was being towed past Atlantic City carrying a load of coke. The leak couldn't be stopped and the barge was lost off of Corson's Inlet.[223]

Sunray Beach, Middle Township, Cape May County. 39° 02' 38" N, 74° 55' 55" W. There is a nature preserve and pier located here. The beaches in this area give us a good idea of what the coast looked like as Europeans first saw it.

Sunset Beach, Lower Township, Cape May County. 38° 56' 58" N, 74° 58' 07" W. 'End of the road' in New Jersey. It is indeed, an ideal place to view sunsets over Delaware Bay. Sunset Beach is the home of the concrete ship "Atlantus" which beached there in 1926.[4] The beach here is well known for producing, Cape May Diamonds, Quartz crystals that can be polished to a brilliant shine.[46]

Sunset Lake, Wildwood Crest, Cape May County. 38° 58' 26" N, 74° 50' 37" W. Along with Turtle Gut, Sunset Lake was once an inlet. These inlets were filled in by area residents in 1910.[41] When one looks out across the lake and the meadows beyond, a wonderful, unobstructed view of the setting sun can be had.

Swainton, Middle Township, Cape May County. 39° 07' 53" N, 74° 46' 39" W. Swainton honors a prominent family of set-tlers in the area. The name is a combining form of the words 'Swain' and 'station'. At one time this area was famous for shipping thousands of barrels of marsh hens to the Philadelphia duck market.[38] Jonathan and Richard Swain came to Cape May County from Long Island, NY in 1706.[138]

Sweetwater, Mullica Township, Atlantic County. 39° 37' 35" N, 74° 38' 58" W. Home of the famous Sweetwater Casino. The restaurant was destroyed in a fire during June, 2008. The ca-sino got its name from its service as a speakeasy (alcohol plus gambling) during Prohibition.[193] Sweetwater is the former name of Pleasant Mills. The name comes from the historical novel, "Kate Aylsford" and is the name of her father's estate.[229]

Swimming Over, Atlantic County. See Leeds Point entry.

Tanners Brook, Galloway Township, Atlantic County. See Oceanville entry.

Taylor Sound, Lower Township, Cape May County. 38° 59' 10" N, 74° 51' 49" W. George Taylor was appointed clerk of the first town meeting held in Cape May County in February

The name Swainton comes from Swain Station.

of 1692. It was Taylor who accused John Jarvis of giving rum to the local Indians at his home. Jarvis didn't deny it and was convicted.[136, 137]

The Villas, Lower Township, Cape May County. See Villas entry.

Thompsontown, Hamilton Township, Atlantic County. 39° 24' 59" N, 74° 42' 32" W. This hamlet was located just south of Gravelly Run.[76] The Thompsons were a prominent family in Atlantic County. Their ranks included a judge, physician, mayor, military officers and they were proprietors of a general store here in early times.[71, 73]

Tilton Road, Hamilton Township, Egg Harbor Township, Pleasantville and Northfield, Atlantic County. 39° 22' 36" N, 74° 33'14" W. Named after an early area developer.[40]

Town Bank, Lower Township, Cape May County. 38° 59' 15" N, 74° 57'12" W. Town Bank was visited by Henry Hudson in his ship Half Moon in 1609. The Half Moon was anchored off-shore while observations were made by crew member Robert Juet.[25] Town Bank is located on a high, sand bank overlooking Delaware Bay.[187] Settled by whalers from Long Island, NY and other parts of New England, it is the first town to exist on the cape.[114] The whalers were attracted by the seasonal whaling in Delaware Bay. At one time, the Town Bank area was also home to another group of whalers, the Lenni Lenape Indians. Records show that the Kechemeche Tribe, led by King Nummy, preceded the New Englanders. The historic record states that the Indians sold a whale to a European settler in 1635.[30] Town Bank was originally called Portsmouth as well as New England Village. Before it became Town Bank, it was called Cape May Town, Coxe Hall and Falmouth.[46, 74]

Townsend's Inlet, Cape May County. Town. 39° 07' 35" N, 74° 42' 41" W. Townsend's Inlet is named for John Townsend who came to Cape May County in the late 1600s. Townsend was a Quaker and was fleeing the New York Colony where he had been banished for aiding dissidents. He built a mill on Magnolia Lake in Dennis Township.[34]

Townsend's Inlet, Cape May County. Inlet. 39° 07' 04" N, 74° 42' 52" W. This waterway is named for the John Townsend family, early settlers of the area.[34] See Oceanview entry.

Tuckahoe, Upper Township, Cape May County. 39° 17' 24" N, 74° 45' 14" W. Tuckahoe is derived from a Lenni Lenape Indian tribe word, meaning, "Where the deer are shy and hard to approach."[34] This town was once known as Williamsburg.[119] The first white man to settle in Tuckahoe was pioneer John Mackey.[138]

Tuckahoe River, Atlantic/Cape May Counties. 39° 17' 41" N, 74° 38' 40" W. This river separates Atlantic and Cape May counties. Derived from a Lenni Lenape Indian tribe word, meaning, "Where the deer are shy and hard to approach".[34] A sub division of the Lenni Lenape, the Tuckahoes, lived along this river.[46] A map of Cape May County in 1723 refers to the river as Turkey Hoe.[149]

Turtle Gut, Middle Township, Cape May County. 38° 56' 58" N, 74° 58' 07" W. A Revolutionary War battle was fought just offshore when two British warships boarded the brigantine, *Nancy.* 50 British sailors were killed, victims of a booby trap that resulted in a huge explosion.[46] Along with Sunset Lake, Turtle Gut, was once an inlet. They were filled in by area residents in 1910.[41]

Two-Mile Beach, Cape May County. 38° 56' 53" N, 74° 51' 41" W. Two-Mile Beach is located on the extreme southwest end of Five Mile Beach. It is approximately two miles long depending on where you start and end measurement. Currently, the US Coast Guard holds this area as a reservation. See Cold Spring Harbor entry.

Upper Township, Cape May County. 39° 12' 30" N, 74° 42' 15" W (Seaville). In 1723 Cape May County was divided into three precincts, Upper, Middle and Lower. When the townships of Cape May County are viewed on a map, Upper Township is at the top, Middle Townshi is in the middle and Lower Township is at the bottom. Upper Township incorporated in 1798, and is one of the state's original 104 townships.[103] Both Dennis Township and Ocean City were created from portions of Upper Township.[102]

Venice Park, Atlantic City, Atlantic County. 39° 22' 35" N, 74° 26' 43" W. Anyone who has visited here has taken note of the many waterfront homes on Venice Lagoon and the shore line of this island. It was home to the famous Inlet Club and its annual clam bake. The author once attended that event and noticed several broken cases of dinnerware from the Captain Starn's Restaurant discarded on the broken concrete shoreline. The deep blue pattern and sailboat on the plates was very distinctive and memorable.

Ventnor, Atlantic County. 39° 20' 25" N, 74° 28' 39" W. Ventnor is named after the town of Ventnor, England.[105] Named by Mrs. S. Bartram Richards in 1889. Two streets on Absecon Island recall her contribution, Bartram Place in Atlantic City and Richards Avenue, Ventnor. Ventnor, England is actually located on the south coast of Britain's Isle of Wight.[124] Take note of the English Tudor style of construction of the historic Ventnor city hall. Ventnor is situated on Absecon Island between Atlantic City and Margate. The boardwalk continues on from Atlantic City through Ventnor to the boundary with Margate at Fredericksburg Avenue. Ventnor was once known as South Atlantic City.[77]

Ventnor Heights, Ventnor, Atlantic County. 39° 20' 58" N, 74° 29' 05" W. This section of Ventnor City was sometimes referred to as "Plywood Palace" by locals. At one point in its growth, plywood construction methods were widely employed. In the eyes of some old timers this was inferior to the then traditional framing and sheathing materials. Compare to today's building materials. This is a lovely and authentic section of Jersey Shore life that is surrounded on water by three sides.

It lies to the North of Ventnor proper and in that sense it is 'higher' although its average elevation is considerably lower.

Villas, Lower Township, Cape May County. 39° 01' 43" N, 74° 56' 19" W. Villas is also called The Villas. Developers of the Villas called it a "retirement haven". Another area town, North Cape May, was referred to as "the St. Petersburg of the North," And then there's Miami Beach (Cape May County), also referencing a well-known retirement Mecca.[213] One can imagine how "a little _villa_ to settle down in," would be attractive to retirees. Originally, the developer called it Wildwood Villas.[80]

Walkers Forge, Hamilton Township, Atlantic County. 39° 26' 49" N, 74° 45' 04" W. Named for Lewis M. Walker an ironmaster and Atlantic County's first assemblyman.[180]

Wesley Avenue, Ocean City, Cape May County. 39° 17' 05" N, 74° 33' 56" W. Ocean City was founded by Methodists. Wesley Avenue was named for one of those founders.[40]

West Atlantic City, Egg Harbor Township, Atlantic County. 39° 22' 40" N, 74° 29' 22" W. The town's name derives from a train station, "West Atlantic" on the Shore Fast Line of The West Jersey and Seashore railroad.[200] At one time, West Atlantic City was home to Oxford Academy, a private boarding school for the rich and famous. The author recalls driving past this gated facility whose main building gave the appearance of The White House. It is the former home of Benjamin Fox who developed the town. The famous Ventnor Boat Works also was located here, as well as, "The Log Restaurant" (which had a façade in the shape of a horizontal tree trunk), "Ben's Bar-B-Que" and "The Drums Restaurant" who advertised, "You can't beat the drums."[199]

West Cape May, Borough of, Cape May County. 38° 56' 19' N, 74° 56' 31" W. The first Europeans on the cape settled here. They were whalers. West Cape May was referred to on early maps as Eldredge. In 1880, a goldbeaters business was established and made gold leaf for bibles. This area was settled before Sea Grove (Cape May Point) and Cape Island (Cape May City).[175]

West Wildwood, Borough of, Cape May County. 39° 00' 08" N, 74° 49' 28" W. Only .3 of a mile square, it is linked to Wildwood at Maple Avenue by a two-lane bridge, the only access to this community. It was founded as a resort by Warren Hann who was the grandson of one of the county's early glass manufacturers. In the late 1890s he invested in land west of Five Mile Beach that was separated by an inlet. A casino was once located here.[176]

Weymouth, Atlantic County. 39° 30' 54" N, 74° 46' 44" W. Named after Weymouth, England.[169] A former stop on the stage line from Great Egg Harbor (the original Egg Harbor Township) to Philadelphia.[157, 171]

Weymouth Furnace, Hamilton Township, Atlantic County. 39° 31' 06" N, 74° 46' 44" W. An early 19th Century iron furnace along the headwaters of the Egg Harbor River. It cast cannon and ball for the War of 1812. It was known as the Weymouth Iron Works.[47] It is now a county park.

Weymouth Township, Atlantic County. 39° 25' 30" N, 74° 47' 29" W. Weymouth, or Waymouth, is a Quaker name and was applied to their holdings here in the days of Charles II.[115] Weymouth Township separated from Egg Harbor Township in 1798.[52] Another possible explanation for the name comes from the fact that Weymouth, England is a large port on that country's southern coast. It was a common place for immigrants to depart for the New World. Weymouth incorporated in 1798 and was mentioned in Gloucester County records as early as 1694.[2]

Whale Beach, Strathmere, Upper Township, Cape May County. 39° 11' 18" N, 74° 39' 43" W. According to local sports journalist, Lou Rodia, this place gets its name from the frequent sightings of whales from the beach many years ago. Whale Creek derived its name from this beach.[19] Early site of whaling activity and whale strandings.[34] Located on Ludlam Beach.

Whale Creek, Strathmere, Upper Township, Cape May County. 39° 11' 13" N, 74° 40' 16" W. Whale Creek takes its name from Whale Beach which is located on the ocean side of Strathmere.[19] Located on Ludlam Beach.

White Horse Pike, Atlantic County. 39° 26' 20" N, 74° 31' 06" W. This road is an historic, major, state highway that runs through Hammonton, Galloway Township, Absecon, and Atlantic City. One explanation for its name says that a white horse played a prominent role in the dedication ceremony for this road in 1921. This was described in the Gazette Review newspaper edition of June 30 of that year. Another origin is suggested by James Steelman in a letter to the editor of The Press, Atlantic City, of November, 16, 1994. Mr. Steelman claims his father, Fred Steelman, stated that the road was named after the White Horse Tavern in Somerdale, NJ. The elder Steelman was employed as a road engineer at the time of the ceremony. This old tavern was established in 1739 and unfortunately was demolished in 1966.[20]

Whitesboro, Middle Township, Cape May County. 39° 02' 20" N, 74° 51' 25" W. Named after Henry White, US Congressman.[170]

Wildwood, City of, Cape May County. 38° 59' 20" N, 74° 48' 17" W. Wildwood was formerly known as the fishing village of Holly Beach Borough.[13, 33] Wildwood is located on Five Mile Beach and is named for the wind-formed, crooked shrubs, bushes and trees that once characterized the vegetation of this locale.[32]

Wildwood was originally called Holly Beach.

Wildwood Crest, Cape May County. 38° 58' 29" N, 74° 50' 01" W. Johnathan Swain purchased this land from King George I in 1717. The famous battle of Turtle Gut occurred off Wildwood Crest on June 29, 1776. The British warship Kingfisher engaged the brigantine Nancy and the frigates Lexington and Wasp.[177] Named for an abundance of wild flowers.[171]

Wildwood Villas, Lower Township, Cape May County. See Villas entry.

Williamsburg, Upper Township, Cape May County. See Tuckahoe entry.

Wills Creek, Lower Township, Cape May County. See Bidwell Creek entry.

Woodbine, Borough, Cape May County. 39° 13' 59" N, 74° 48' 37" W. Woodbine was founded as a haven for Eastern European Jews in 1891.[120] The local chamber of commerce tells us that Woodbine means, Honeysuckle and indicates a bond of love.[121] Known to be home to prolific moonshine operations during Prohibition.[149]

Zion Road, Egg Harbor Township, Atlantic County. 39° 22' 01" N, 74° 35' 16" W. Named for the Zion Church located there.[40]

Glossary

- **Bayou**

  ❖ A creek, secondary watercourse, or minor river that is tributary to another body of water.

- **Brigantine**

  ❖ An ancient sailing ship that has two, square-rigged masts.

- **Gut**

  ❖ A narrow waterway or small creek.

- **Hammock**

  ❖ A fertile area in the southern U.S. and especially Florida that is usually higher than its surroundings and that is characterized by hardwood vegetation and deep humus-rich soil.

- **Neck**

  ❖ "A narrow stretch of land."

- **Run**

  ❖ A small stream; brook; rivulet.[201]

- **Sound**

  ❖ A long broad inlet of the ocean generally parallel to the coast.

- **Thoroughfare** (Thorofare)

  ❖ "A way or place for passage."

- **Township**

  ❖ "A unit of local government in some northeastern … states usually having a chief administrative officer."

➢ Please note that all definitions are from "Dictionary and Thesaurus-Merriam-Webster Online." **http://www. meriam-webster.com/** February 7, 2010 and *Merriam-Websters Collegiate Dictionary, Tenth Edition.*

∽✺ ∽✺ ∽✺

Works Cited

1 - Camp, D. (1989, March 30-April 5). Channel Dredging Planned for Bay. The Advisor.

2 - Powell, C. (1992, November 19). What's in a name, Town Titles in Atlantic County Stem From History. Right Where You Live. This Week, Atlantic County.

3 - "Did You Know?" Atlantic City Press, April, 1989. Absecon Beach entry.

3.5 - "Did You Know?" Atlantic City Press, April, 1989. Brigantine entry.

3.75 - "Brigantine – Definition from the Merriam-Webster Online Dictionary." http://www.merriam-webster.com/dictionary/brigantine.

4 - Cape May County tourism literature. 1988.

5 - "'Cape Island': semi-historical blend of Cape May, Civil War." Jacob Schaad Jr. The Press, Atlantic City, NJ, July 29, 1990, C-11.

6 - "The Chronicle of Historic Cold Spring Village." Volume 2, Number 1. Summer 1988.

7 - Reserved.

7.5 - Author's visits to Corson's Inlet.

8 - "Reader Traces Origin of Delilah Road." –Rob Laymon, The Press, Atlantic City, NJ, September 3, 1994

9 - "Early History of Atlantic County, NJ." Reprint of 1915 Edition. Lavinia, Willis, Balliet & Fish, Eds. Atlantic City Press 1988 notice of publication.

10 - "Visiting Salesmen Always Welcome in Southern N.J." William McMahon. The Press, Atlantic City, NJ. October 22, 1989.

11 - "Ferry boats paddle along for 300 years." William McMahon. The Press, Atlantic City, NJ. July 30, 1989.

12 - "Did you Know?" Atlantic City Press, May 1989. Little Egg Harbor Inlet entry.

13 - "A Tour of the Past Puts County's Present in Perspective." Jennifer Shaub, The Press, Atlantic City, NJ. August 12, 1993.

14 - "Upper hasn't ignored erosion in Strathmere," Voice of the People, The Press, Atlantic City, NJ. November 23, 2007.

15 - "Shore Thing," Atlantic City Press, date unknown.

16 - "Ohio blast injures 42," Michael Fleming. "This Week." Atlantic City Press.

17 - "Did You Know?" AC Press, circa 1989. Simon Lake entry.

18 - "Antique map restored in Somers Point... ." EHN/ACR/MJ, January 19, 1989

19 - "Adopted Whale, Salt, Rises Off New Jersey." The Press, Atlantic City, NJ, February 19, 1995.

20 - "White Horse Pike Named After Tavern." The Press, Atlantic City, NJ. November 16, 1994.

21 - Lavinia, Willis, Balliet & Fish 72.

22 - "Atlantic County, New Jersey." Street Map Book. Alexandria Drafting Company, Alexandria, VA. 2002. P. 68.

23 - "Abandoned and little-Known Airfields: New Jersey: Atlantic City area." http://www.members.tripod.com/airfields_freeman/NJ/Airfields_NJ_AtlanticCity.html

24 - "Stories of Mays Landing." Dr. Ralph K. Turp. South Jersey Magazine, 1981-83. P.8.

25 - "Sailors, Whalers and Settlers." The Press, Explorer, August 20, 2007.

26 - "Over time, Little Beach Island went to birds." The Press, Atlantic City, NJ. September 24, 2007.

27 - "Unique trolley attracts visitors to Brigantine." The Press, Atlantic City, NJ. Historical Walk, William McMahon.

28 - "Picture the Past in Port Republic." Then and Now, William McMahon. The Press, Atlantic City, NJ., January 28, 1990.

29 - "The Dead Among Us," Arthur Schwerdt. The Sandpaper, October 27, 1989.

30 - "Whalers, New Museum tells story of settlers descending on Cape to hunt for oil." Richard Degener. The Press, Atlantic City, NJ., August 16, 1988.

31 - "History of Egg Harbor Township: McKee City." Around The Township , circa 1990.

32 - "Wildwoods out to put meaning back in name." Thomas Barlas. The Press, Atlantic City, NJ, February 26, 1990.

33 - "'Wild Life' once meant trees in Wildwood." Thomas Barlas. The Press, Atlantic City, NJ, February 26, 1990.

34 - "From Skunk Sound to Drag Island region's names offer history, folklore." Richard Degener, Tom Davis, Aisling Swift. The Press, Atlantic City, NJ, January 8, 1996.

35 - Conversation with William Killian, June14, 2008.

36 - Author.

37 - "Historical trust funds allotted." William McMahon. The Press of Atlantic City, NJ, June 3, 1990.

38 - "Islands in the Stream". Arthur Schwerdt. The Sandpaper, October 20, 1989.

39 - Absecon Island. November 24, 2009. Retrieved from Wikipedia: http://en.wikipedia.org/wiki/Absecon_Island

40 - "A road by any other name." Marjorie Donchey. The Press of Atlantic City NJ, August 30, 1994.

41 - Sunny Day (magazine, tourist literature).

42 - "Swamp," The Press, Atlantic City, March 6, 1988.

43 - "O.C. silt threatens boaters." The Press, Atlantic City, NJ, March 3, 1989.

44 - "Chestnut Neck is burning, October 6, 1778." Franklin W. Kemp. The Scanner, August, 1988.

45 - "Variety Spices up fishing action in Delaware Bay," Mike Shepherd. The Press, Atlantic City, NJ, August 14, 1988.

46 - "A Historic Tour of Cape May County." Cape May County Department of Public Affairs.

47 - "Did You Know?" The Press, Atlantic City, NJ. Weymouth Furnace entry.

48 - "Paper, cotton helped build Pleasant Mills." Historical Walk. William McMahon. The Press, Atlantic City, NJ, January 14, 1990.

49 - Atlantic City NJ. November 7, 2009. Retrieved from Wikipedia: http://en.wikipedia.org/wiki/Atlantic_City_NJ

50 - Genealogy Quest. New Jersey (and Pennsylvania) Place Names September, 4, 2008. http://www.genealogy-quest.com/collections/njplace.html.

51 - September 6, 2008. Atlantic County. Retrieved from Get NJ-The Origin of New Jersey Place Names: http://www.getnj.com/origname/orignamea.shtml

52 - "History and Historic Places: Atlantic County NJ - NJGenWeb." http://www.rootsweb.ancestry.com/~njatlant/history.html#history2" November 7, 2009.

53 - Get NJ-The Origin of New Jersey Place Names. Avalon.

54 - Avalon History http://www.avalonboro.org/pictures/histor3.gif September 6, 2008.

55 - "Historic American Buildings Survey." http://memory.loc.gov/cgi September 9, 2008.

56- "Sketches of Egg Harbor Township." http://www.eht.com/history/Sketches/bargaintown/index.htm September 9, 2008.

57 - USGS, GNIS, Beck, Henry Charlton. Forgotten Towns of Southern New Jersey. New Brunswick, New Jersey: E.P. Dutton & Co., 1936; Rutgers University Press, 1961. Fourteenth printing, 1994. Map 42. http://geonames.usgs.gov/pls/

gnispublic/f?p=115:4:16552888129084135753::NO:4:P4_FID, FNAME:874937%2CLudleys%20Beach September 10, 2008.

58 - Delaware Bay. November 12, 2009. Retrieved from Wikipedia: http://en.wikipedia.org/wiki/Delaware_Bay

59 - Get NJ – The Origin of New Jersey Place Names. Pomona.

60 - Get NJ – The Origin of New Jersey Place Names. Belleplain, Brigantine Beach Island, Brigantine City, Cologne, Conovertown, Delaware Bay.

60.1 - "Brigantine Beach NJ History." http://www.brigantine-beachnj.com/history.html November 6, 2009.

61 - "Cape May County History: Dennis Township." **http://www.cmmuseum.org/history/dennis.htm** October 7, 2008.

62 - "History of Cape May County." **http://members.tripod.com/scott_mcgonigle/history.htm#lost** October 9, 2008.

63 - Get NJ – The Origin of New Jersey Place Names. Hereford Inlet. **http://www.getnj.com/origname/orignameh.shtml**

64 - Get NJ – The Origin of New Jersey Place Names. Lake Lenape. **http://www.getnj.com/origname/orignamel.shtml**

65 - Get NJ – The Origin of New Jersey Place Names. Margate. **http://www.getnj.com/origname/orignamem.shtml**

66 - Eric Palsson Mullica: Information from Answers.com **http://www.answers.com/topic/eric_p-lsson-mullica**

67 - Reserved.

68 - Get NJ – The Origin of New Jersey Place Names. Anglesea. **http://www.getnj.com/origname/orignamea.shtml**

69 - Turp 10.

70 - Reserved.

71 - Turp 71.

72 - BVT History. November 28, 2009. Retrieved from: http:// www.buenavistatownship.org/bvt_history.htm

73 - Turp 26.

74 - Historic South Jersey Towns. 1964. William McMahon. Press Publishing Company, Atlantic City, NJ. P. 250.

75 - Bader Field. November 3, 2009. Retrieved from Wikipedia: http://en.wikipedia.org/wiki/Bader Field New_Jersey

76 - Historical Atlantic County, New Jersey Maps. December 1, 2009. Retrieved from: http://mapmaker.rutgers.edu/1872atlas/ AtlanticCounty1872.jpg.

77 - McMahon 249.

78 - McMahon 47.

79 - U.S. Highway 40. May 29, 2009. Retrieved from Wikipedia: http://en.wikipedia.org/wiki/U.S._Highway_40

80 - "Group hopes to restore charm of 1888 schoolhouse in Lower." Richard Degener. The Press, Atlantic City, NJ, December 22, 2009.

81 - Cape May, New Jersey. November 24, 2009. Retrieved from Wikipedia: http://en.wikipedia.org/wiki/ Cape_May_New_Jersey

82 - "Bader Field, The History." May 31, 2009. http://www.authors-den.com/visit/viewarticle.asp?AuthorID=941248id=43550

83 - New Jersey Route 47. July 1, 2009. Retrieved from Wikipedia: http://wikipedia.org/wiki/New Jersey_Route_47

84 - Rio Grande NJ. July 1, 2009. Retrieved from Wikipedia: http://wikipedia.org/wiki/Rio_Grande_(NJ)

85 - "Map of Longport and Oberon." Early map printed in the Press of Atlantic City. Date unknown.

86 - "New Jersey, a guide to its Present and Past." Google Books. July 1, 2009.

87 - "Five Mile Beach." Great Vacation. Wildwood NJ .Com. http://www.greatvacationwildwoodnj.com/wildwood/ wildwoodhistory.html July 1, 2009.

88 - USGS, GNIS, "Five Mile Beach." Beck, Henry Charlton. Forgotten Towns of Southern New Jersey. New Brunswick, New Jersey: E.P. Dutton & Co., 1936; Rutgers University Press, 1961. Fourteenth printing, 1994. Map 42. http://geonames. usgs.gov/pls/gnispublic/f?p=116:4:337285432922406::NO:4:p4_ FID,FNAME:882:649%2CFive%20Miles%Beach July 1, 2009.

89 - "Seven Mile Beach." USGS GNIS. http://geonames. usgs.gov/pls/gnispublic/f?p=116:4:337285432922406::NO::P3_ FID,P3_TITLE:880479%2CSeven%20Mile%Beach July 1, 2009.

90 - Lower Township New Jersey. July 15, 2009. Retrieved from Wikipedia: http://wikipedia.org/wiki/Lower_Township,_NJ

91 - "History of Weymouth Township by Stephen Csere." http:// www.weymouthnj.org/recent_weymouth_township_htm July 2, 2009.

92 - Reserved.

93 - Lavinia, Willis, Balliet & Fish 96.

94 - Lavinia, Willis, Balliet & Fish 92.

95 - Linwood, New Jersey. November 20, 2009. Retrieved from Wikipedia: http://wikipedia.org/wiki/Linwood,_NJ

96 - "Upper Township, Cape May County, New Jersey (NJ) Detailed Profile." City-Data.com http://www.city-data.com/township/Upper-Cape-May-NJ.html July 5, 2009.

97 - "Sunset Beach Cape May New Jersey." http://www.capemay.com/Editorial/october05/sunsetbeach2.html July 6, 2009.

98 - "History of Cape May Point-The Early Years." http://www.cmpnj.com/history.html

99 - Cape May Point, New Jersey. July 9, 2009. Retrieved from Wikipedia: http://en.wikipedia.org/wiki/Cape_May_Point_NJ

100 - Ducktown, Atlantic City. July 13, 2009. Retrieved from Wikipedia: http://wikipedia.org/wiki/Ducktown

101 - Middle Township, New Jersey. July 15, 2009. Retrieved from Wikipedia: _http://wikipedia.org/wiki/Middle_Township,_NJ

102 - Upper Township, New Jersey. July 15, 2009. Retrieved from Wikipedia: _http://wikipedia.org/wiki/Upper_Township_New_Jersey

103 - History of Cape May County NJ. July 15, 2009. http://www.thejerseycape.net/historic/county_history.htm

104 - Sewell, William Joyce – Biographical Information. January 26, 2010, Retrieved from http://bioguide.congress.gov/scripts/biodisplay.pl?index=s000262

105 - Get NJ – The Origin of New Jersey Place Names. **http://www.getnj.com/origname/orignamev.shtml**

106 - "Atlantic County Government Division of Parks and Recreation." http://www.aclink.org/PARKS/mainpages/historic.asp July 27, 2009.

107 - "The wild coast-exploring the … ." Google. http://www.books.google.com/books?id=CICs38ekWqcC&pg=PA17&lpg=PA17&dq=bennets+bog+nj&source=bl&ots=55bvXv9BEy&sig=j62oZ99pv1M5SR8uqPTUnv-i3lk&hl=en&e=A-ttSvH4NcLhlAf9u621Ag&sa=X8oi=book_result&ct=result&resnum=8 July 27, 2009.

108 - The history of Cape May County, New Jersey: fr…. July 28, 2009. http://www.archive.org/stream/historyofcapemay01stev#page/46/mode/1up

109 - Lavinia, Willis, Balliet & Fish 91.

110 - Lavinia, Willis, Balliet & Fish 167.

111 - 100 Birds and How They Got Their Names. 2002. Diana Wells. Algonquin Books of Chapel Hill, Chapel Hill, NC. P. xv.

112 - Lavinia, Willis, Balliet & Fish 169.

113 - Egg Harbor Township Tercentenary Publications Committee 77-79.

114 - Cape May History-NJ. July 31, 2009. Retrieved from: http://www.usgennet.org/usa/nj/county/capemay/Cape%20May%20City.htm

115 - "Weymouth History." http://www.weymouthnj.org/weymouth_history.htm August 1, 2009.

116 - "Mullica Township, New Jersey." Wikipedia _http://wikipedia.org/wiki/Mullica_Township,_New_Jersey August 2, 2009.

117 – "Which beach is THE beach?" CapeMay.com Online Magazine http://www.ask.com/web?q=how+did+poverty+beach+get+its+name&search=&qsrc=0&o=0&l=dirMay25, 2010.

118 - "Which beach is THE beach?" Cape May Magazine Online http://capemay.com/magazine/2009/07/which-beach-is-the-beach/ August 2, 2009.

119 - "Upper Township." http://www.uppertownship.com/City_Hall/yesterday.html August 2, 2009.

120 - Woodbine, New Jersey. August 3, 2009. Retrieved from Wikipedia: http://wikipedia.org/wiki/Woodbine,_New_Jersey

121 - "Greater Woodbine Chamber of Commerce". http://www.wcnj.org/wcwoodbinehistory.html August 3, 2009.

122 - "The Township of Mullica." http://www.mullicatownship.org/about_mullica.aspx?AspxAutoDetectCookieSupport+1 August 5, 2009.

123 - "HIKING PLEASANT MILLS." http://www.nynjctbotany.org/njoptofc/plsntmil.html August 5, 2009.

124 - Ventnor City, New Jersey. August 6, 2009. Retrieved from Wikipedia: http://www.en.wikipedia.org/wiki/Ventnor_City_New_jersey

125 - "Jersey Shore guide>>Ludlam Island & Sea Isle City early History." http://www.jerseyshoreguide.net/sea-isle-city-early-history/#more-146 August 6, 2009.

126 - Sea Isle City, New Jersey. August 6, 2009. Retrieved from Wikipedia: http://www.en.wikipedia.org/wiki/Sea_Isle_CityNew_Jersey

127 - "Cape May Higbee Beach." http://www.capemay.com/Editorial/june08/HigbeeBeach.htm August 8, 2009.

128 - Goshen, New Jersey. August 9, 2009. Retrieved from Wikipedia: http://www.en.wikipedia.org/wiki/Goshen_New_Jersey

129 - Get NJ – The Origin of New Jersey Place Names. **http://www.getnj.com/origname/orignameg.shtml**

130 - McMahon 109.

131 - Reserved.

132 - The history of Cape May County, New Jersey: fr... http://www.archive.org/stream/historyofcapemay01stev#page/39/mode/1up

133 - "Get NJ-Historic Roadsides-Cape May County." http://www.getnj.com/historicroadsides/capemay.shtml August 11, 2009.

134 - The history of Cape May County, New Jersey: fr... http://www.archive.org/stream/historyofcapemay01stev#page/41/mode/1up

135 - The history of Cape May County, New Jersey: fr... http://www.archive.org/stream/historyofcapemay01stev#page/43/mode/1up

136 - The history of Cape May County, New Jersey: fr... http://www.archive.org/stream/historyofcapemay01stev#page/47/mode/1up

137 - The history of Cape May County, New Jersey: fr... http://
www.archive.org/stream/historyofcapemay01stev#page/48/
mode/1up

138 - The history of Cape May County, New Jersey: fr... http://
www.archive.org/stream/historyofcapemay01stev#page/54/
mode/1up

139 - The history of Cape May County, New Jersey: fr... http://
www.archive.org/stream/historyofcapemay01stev#page/68/
mode/1up

140 - The history of Cape May County, New Jersey: fr... http://
www.archive.org/stream/historyofcapemay01stev#page/
141/mode/1up

141 - Dorwart, J. 1992. Cape May County, New Jersey: the
making of an American resort community. Rutgers University
Press, New brunswick, P. 102.

142 - The history of Cape May County, New Jersey: fr... http://
www.archive.org/stream/historyofcapemay01stev#page/
224/mode/1up

143 - The history of Cape May County, New Jersey: fr... http://
www.archive.org/stream/historyofcapemay01stev#page/
259/mode/1up

144 - The history of Cape May County, New Jersey: fr... http://
www.archive.org/stream/historyofcapemay01stev#page/
265/mode/1up

145 - The history of Cape May County, New Jersey: fr... http://
www.archive.org/stream/historyofcapemay01stev#page/
377/mode/1up

146 - East Jersey. August 24, 2009. Retrieved from Wikipedia:
http://www.en.wikipedia.org/wiki/East_Jersey

147 - Get NJ-The Origin of New Jersey Place Names. Mays Landing. http://www.getnj.com/origname/orignamem.shtml

148 - "Brief History of Ocean City, NJ" http://www.ocnjmuseum.org/reference/brief_history.htm August 26, 2009

149 - Dorwart 31, 154.

150 - Encyclopedia of New Jersey. August 28,2009. Retrieved from: http://books.google.com/books?id=r9Ni6_u0JEC&pg =PA590&lpg=PA590&dq=naming+ottens+harbor+nj&sourc e=bl&ots=98&IPEnxuIR&sig=InOOHtrbU_koIs9Mhg0NPUyJPs &hl=en&ei=cvCXSuSDMM_0IAfk9rykBQ&sa=X&oi=book_res ult&ct=result&resnum==3#v=onepage&q=&f=false

151 - Lavinia, Willis, Balliet & Fish 126.

152 - Lavinia, Willis, Balliet & Fish 149.

153 - Lavinia, Willis, Balliet & Fish 156.

154 - Lavinia, Willis, Balliet & Fish 161.

155 - Get NJ-The Origin of New Jersey Place Names. Folsom. http://www.getnj.com/origname/orignamef.shtml August 31, 2008.

156 - Lavinia, Willis, Balliet & Fish 162.

157 - Lavinia, Willis, Balliet & Fish 164.

158 - Lavinia, Willis, Balliet & Fish 169.

159 - Lavinia, Willis, Balliet & Fish 168.

160 - "BVT History." http://www.buenavistatownship.org/ bvt_history.htm September 10, 2009.

161 - "Points of Interest-Cape May County Chamber of Commerce Visitor Information." http://www.cape-maycountychamber.com/visitor/points-of-interest.htm September 12, 2009.

162 - "Unofficial 'mayor of Penny Pot happy to serve public-press of Atlantic City.com" http://www.pressofatlantic-city.com/news/press/atlantic/article_7af22ca6-b429-5829-bc24-64ae738b10df.html September 14, 2009.

163 - "Strathmere – a brief history& vintage photos." http://www.strathmere.net/1.html September 14, 2009.

164 - Landisville, New Jersey. September 15, 2009. Retrieved from Wikipedia: http://en.wikipedia.org/wiki/Landisville,_New_Jersey

165 - Marven Gardens. September 16, 2009. Retrieved from Wikipedia: http://en.wikipedia.org/wiki/Marven_Gardens

166 - Get NJ-The Origin of New Jersey Place Names. Mizpah http://www.getnj.com/origname/orignamem.shtml

167 - Get NJ-The Origin of New Jersey Place Names. Head-of-the-River. http://www.getnj.com/origname/orignameh.shtml

168 - Get NJ-The Origin of New Jersey Place Names. Nummytown. http://www.getnj.com/origname/origna-men.shtml

169 - Get NJ-The Origin of New Jersey Place Names. Weymouth, Whitesboro, Wildwood. http://www.getnj.com/origname/orignamew.shtml
170 - Dorwart 117.

171 - Egg Harbor Township Tercentenary Publications 1.

172 - Laurie, M. and Mappen, M. 2008. "Encyclopedia of New Jersey." Rutgers University Press, New Brunswick, NJ P. 104.

173 - Laurie and Mappen 170.

174 - Laurie and Mappen 588.

175 - Laurie and Mappen 862.

176 - Laurie and Mappen 865.

177 - Laurie and Mappen 872.

178 - "Wilson's Biography." http://xroads.virginia.edu/~public/wilson/bio.html February 4, 2010.

179 - Get NJ - The Origin of New Jersey Place Names. Longport. getnj.com/origname/orignamel.shtml

180 - Get NJ - The Origin of New Jersey Place Names. Walkers Forge. getnj.com/origname/orignamew.shtml

181 - Hammonton, New Jersey. October 24, 2009. Retrieved from Wikipedia: http://en.wikipedia.org/wiki/Hammonton,_New_Jersey

182 - "Official website of Galloway Township, New Jersey." http://www.gallowaytwp-NJ.gov/index.php?id-0&view=about October 24, 2009.

183 - New Jersey Route 48. October 23, 2009. Retrieved from Wikipedia: http://www.en.wikipedia.org/wiki/New_Jersey_Route_48

184 - "Ask.com – New Jersey Conservation Foundation." http://www.ask.com/bar?q=who+was+lake%27s+bay+nj+

named+after&page=18qsrc=08dm=all&ab=0&title=New+J
ersey+Conservation+Foundation&u=http%3A%2F%2Fwww.
njconservation.org%2Fhtml%2Fpreserves%2Flakesbay.htm&
sg=miKYXdBEAR%2FKcPBtnpD0%2B5duoAwuoyxZbOplBbm
JQho%30%tsp=1256849109125 October 29, 2009.

185 - "Ventnor Boat Works." http://www.vintageboatinglife.
com/Default.web/default803.htm October 29, 2009.

186 - GET NJ – Historic Roadsides – Cape May County. http://
www.getnj.com/histicroadsides/capemay.shtml

187 - "New Jersey State Library." http://www.njstatelib.org-
NJ_Information-Digital_Collections_Place_Names-PLACE.
pdf November 1, 2009.

188 - "ABOUT OUR TOWN." http://www.buenavistatown-
ship.org/about_our_town.htm#profile%20and%20History
November 1, 2009.

189 - Richland, New Jersey. November 1, 2009. Retrieved
from   Wikipedia: http://www.en.wikipedia.org/wiki/
Richland,_New_Jersey

190 - "City of Northfield, New Jersey." http://www.cityof-
northfield.org/main/about.asp November 1, 2009.

191 - "History of Linwood." http://www.linwoodnj.org/
LinHisTxt.html#anchor1951978 November 2, 2009.

192 - "A Brief Time Line History of Absecon." http://www.
westfieldnj.com/whs/history/Counties/AtlanticCounty/ab-
secon.htm November 2, 2009.

193 - "Fire races through South Jersey restaurant & bar – 6/30/08 –
Philadelphia News – 6abc.com." http://abclocal.go.com/wpv/
story?section=news/local&id=6236543 November 3, 2009.

194 - "Atlantic City Cheers New Train Service." Carlo M. Sardello. New Jersey Living, January/February, 1989. pp. 24–73.

195 - "Origin of Hope Corson Road." "Answer Guy." Atlantic City Press.

196 - Reserved.

197 - "History of Mays Landing." http://www.westfieldnj. com/whs/history/Counties/AtlanticCounty/hamilton.htm November 8, 2009.

198 - The history of Cape May County, New Jersey: fr... http:// www.archive.org/stream/historyofcapemay01stev#page/44/ mode/1up February 4, 2010.

199 - Conversation with Ann Laughlin, Grace McGee and Regina Ireland. November 8, 2009.

200 - Egg Harbor Township Tercentenary Publications Committee 95.

201 - Run. (n.d.) In Dictionary.com. Retrieved from http:// www.dictionary.reference.com/browse/run

202 - The history of Cape May County, New Jersey: fr.... November 9, 2009. http://www.archive.org/stream/ historyofcapemay01stev#page/363/mode/1up

203 - Dorwart 174.

204 - Dorwart, 266.

205 - Dorwart, 149,164.

206 - Dorwart, 216, 232.

207 - Dorwart, 102.

208 - Dorwart, 270, 303.

209 - Dorwart, 198, 235.

210 - Telephone conversation with Tim Kelly, Richard Stockton College Public Relations Officer, November 11, 2009.

211 - Dorwart 114, 128, 269.

212 - Reserved.

213 - Dorwart 243.

214 - Dorwart 29.

215 - Reserved.

216 - "Cape May Beaches, Bed & Breakfast & Lodging – Bacchus Inn B & B NJ." http://www.bacchusinn.com/cape-may.htm November 11, 2009.

217 - U.S. Route 9 – Wikipedia. November 11, 2009. Retrieved from Wikipedia: http://en.wikipedia.org/wiki/U.S._Route_9

218 - Dorwart 96.

219 - "Atlantic City has a long history of marketing to gay community." Lynda Cohen. The Press of Atlantic City, NJ, September 27, 2009.

220 - Copy of map by Beers, Comstock and Cline dated 1872.

221 - "How did Forty Wire Road in Hamilton Township, Atlantic County, get its name?" "The Press Answer Guy." March 2, 2008.

222 - "A glimpse of the past." "Egg Harbor Township Hometown." The Press of Atlantic City, October 21, 2009.

223 - "Wreck of the General Slocum – Historic site safe off Upper Township." Press of Atlantic City, July 10, 2009.

224 - "Where it began." Trudi Gilfillian. Press of Atlantic City, August 24, 2009.

225 - "Answer Guy." Press of Atlantic City, July 12, 2009. Betsy Scull Road entry.

226 - "Has the apostrophe become dispossessed?" Michael Miller. Press of Atlantic City, February 4, 2009.

227 - November 15, 2009. NJ Pine Barrens & Down Jersey: Exploring the history, culture & ecology of South Jersey. Retrieved from: http://www.njpinelandsanddownjersey. com/open/index.php?module=documents&JAS_Document Manager_op+view/Document&JAS_Document_id=262

228 - "Egg Harbor City: NEW GERMANY IN NEW JERSEY." http://www.westjersey.org/ehc_cunz56/ngnj16.htm November 15, 2009.

229 - NJ Pine Barrens & Down Jersey: Exploring the history, culture & ecology of South Jersey." http:// www.njpinelandsanddownjersey.com/open/index.php? module=documents&JAS_DocumentManager_op+view/ Document&JAS_Document_id=147

230 - McMahon 45.

❧ ❧ ❧

Made in the USA
Charleston, SC
16 January 2012